"Your message is deceptively simple yet extraordinarily powerful! If only we'd step back and open our eyes to this reality, we'd be far more successful and have a lot more fun in the process." —Roger J. Dow, V.P., Sales and Marketing, Marriott Corporation

America's top business leaders praise
Soar with Your Strengths
the groundbreaking guide that
shatters long-accepted myths about success

"The Strengths' Theory is a powerful concept. . . . Now we can stop wasting precious time and resources on what we don't do well and zoom in on the strengths of America." —Ed Miller, Ed.D., President and CEO, Future Business Leaders of America/Phi Beta Lambda, Inc.

"A STIMULATING BOOK . . . *Soar with Your Strengths* puts 'strength' in a nutshell."—Philip B. Crosby, President, Career IV Corporation

"VERY ENLIGHTENING...Invaluable for anyone in a management position."—Tom Osborne, Head Football Coach, Nebraska Cornhuskers

"*Soar with Your Strengths* could change the way 16 million small businesses in this country do business. In fact, the Strengths' Theory could be the solution to America's economic turnaround. . . . Clifton and Nelson are definitely on to something that will make a lot of people a lot happier and a lot richer." —Denise Cavenaugh, co-founder, National Association of Women Business Owners

"AN EXCELLENT BOOK—should be recommended reading for any serious student of business." —Bob DeMone, CEO, Canadian Pacific Hotels

SOAR WITH YOUR STRENGTHS

Donald O. Clifton
and
Paula Nelson

A Dell Trade Paperback

A DELL TRADE PAPERBACK

Published by
Dell Publishing
a division of
Bantam Doubleday Dell Publishing Group, Inc.
1540 Broadway
New York, New York 10036

ISBN: 0-440-50564-X

Reprinted by arrangement with Delacorte Press

Printed in the United States of America

Published simultaneously in Canada

January 1996

20   19   18   17   16

BVG

To the source of my strengths—
my wife, Shirley, and our children

D.O.C.

To the source of my strengths—
my mother, Rose

P.E.N.

CONTENTS

SOAR WITH
YOUR STRENGTHS

PART ONE

Let the Rabbits Run:
A Parable

Imagine there is a meadow. In that meadow there is a duck, a fish, an eagle, an owl, a squirrel, and a rabbit. They decide they want to have a school so they can be smart, just like people.

With the help of some grown-up animals, they come up with a curriculum they believe will make a well-rounded animal:

> running,
> swimming,
> tree climbing,
> jumping,
> and flying.

On the first day of school, little br'er rabbit combed his ears, and he went hopping off to his running class.

There he was a star. He ran to the top of the hill and back as fast as he could go, and, oh, did it feel good. He said to himself, "I can't believe it. At school, I get to do what I do best."

The instructor said: "Rabbit, you really have talent for running. You have great muscles in your rear legs. With some training, you will get more out of every hop."

The rabbit said, "I love school. I get to do what I like to do and get to learn to do it better."

The next class was swimming. When the rabbit smelled the chlorine, he said, "Wait, wait! Rabbits don't like to swim."

The instructor said, "Well, you may not like it now, but five years from now you'll know it was a good thing for you."

In the tree-climbing class, a tree trunk was set at a 30-degree angle so all the animals had a chance to succeed. The little rabbit tried so hard he hurt his leg.

In jumping class, the rabbit got along just fine; in flying class, he had a problem. So the teacher gave him a psychological test and discovered he belonged in remedial flying.

In remedial flying class, the rabbit had to practice jumping off a cliff. They told him if he'd just work hard enough, he could succeed.

The next morning, he went on to swimming class. The instructor said, "Today we jump in the water."

"Wait, wait. I talked to my parents about swimming. They didn't learn to swim. We don't like to get wet. I'd like to drop this course."

The instructor said, "You can't drop it. The drop-and-add period is over. At this point you have a choice: Either you jump in or you flunk."

The rabbit jumped in. He panicked! He went down once. He went down twice. Bubbles came up. The instructor saw he was drowning and pulled him out. The other animals had never seen anything quite as funny as this wet rabbit who looked more like a rat without a tail, and so they chirped, and jumped, and barked, and laughed at the rabbit. The rabbit was more humiliated than he had ever been in his life. He wanted desperately to get out of class that day. He was glad when it was over.

He thought that he would head home, that his parents would understand and help him. When he arrived, he said to his parents, "I don't like school. I just want to be free."

"If the rabbits are going to get ahead, you have to get a diploma," replied his parents.

The rabbit said, "I don't want a diploma."

The parents said, "You're going to get a diploma whether you want one or not."

They argued, and finally the parents made the rabbit go to bed. In the morning the rabbit headed off to school with a slow hop. Then he remembered that the principal had said that any time he had a problem to remember that the counselor's door is always open.

When he arrived at school, he hopped up in the chair by the counselor and said, "I don't like school."

And the counselor said, "Mmmm, tell me about it."

And the rabbit did.

The counselor said, "Rabbit, I hear you. I hear you saying you don't like school because you don't like swimming. I think I have diagnosed that correctly. Rabbit, I tell you what we'll do. You're doing just fine in running. I don't know why you need to work on running. What you need to work on is swimming. I'll arrange it so you don't have to go to running anymore, and you can have two periods of swimming."

When the rabbit heard that, he just threw up!

As the rabbit hopped out of the counselor's office, he looked up and saw his old friend, the Wise Old Owl, who cocked his head and said, "Br'er rabbit, life doesn't have to be that way. We could have schools and businesses where people are allowed to concentrate on what they do well."

Br'er rabbit was inspired. He thought when he graduated, he would start a business where the rabbits would do nothing but run, the squirrels could just climb trees, and the fish could just swim. As he disappeared into the meadow, he sighed softly to himself and said, "Oh, what a great place that would be."

CHAPTER I

Let's Fix What's Wrong: A National Obsession

The little rabbit isn't alone.

A quick look around tells the real story: Most companies, schools, families, and organizations function on an unwritten rule:

> *Let's fix what's wrong and let the strengths take care of themselves.*

Like a trap set for a mouse, our national system is rigged to catch people's weaknesses rather than to build on their strengths.

- Business managers spend most of their time working with the weakest performers and zeroing in on mistakes.

- Parents and teachers focus on students' lowest grades rather than on their highest.

- Bankers and credit grantors make credit judgments based on negative credit history.

- Almost all of our country's social work is focused on problems instead of helping people to become self-sufficient.

Why do we continue to focus all our energies on fixing weaknesses while ignoring strengths? Why do we continue to work at some activities without getting much better at them? Why do 80 percent of our New Year's resolutions stay on our lists year after year? Because of faulty reasoning, which is responsible for many a myth in our society.

MYTH #1: FIXING WEAKNESSES WILL MAKE EVERYTHING ALL RIGHT

The popular notion is that if you fix a weakness in an individual, the individual will become stronger; if you correct a weakness in an organization, the organization will become better. Ultimately, one would assume, if all weaknesses were removed or fixed, then everything would be perfect. Sadly, the assumption is false. Fixing weaknesses only puts a person or an organization at normal or average.

Consider the classic example of writing a paper. If all the spelling and syntax mistakes are corrected, will you have created a paper worthy of an A? Wrong. You will have created an error-free paper, but not necessarily an excellent one. Hemingway, Faulkner, and dozens of other important writers are famous for their poor spelling and syntax. Great writing is about transferring the strength of an individual's great thoughts to paper. Once those thoughts are reduced to paper in a clear and orderly fashion, then the spelling mistakes and syntax can be managed by an editor. Excellence can be achieved only by *focusing* on strengths and *managing* weaknesses, not through the elimination of weaknesses.

MYTH #2: LET THE STRENGTHS TAKE CARE OF THEMSELVES

If a person excels at something, say selling, math problems, motivating people, or designing interiors, an interesting knee-jerk reaction occurs: We take those strengths for granted. The assumption seems to be that strengths will naturally develop. The common thinking goes that if you really want to grow, don't waste time working on the things you're already good at; instead work on your weak areas so you can develop to your fullest.

With the exception of the arts and sports, strengths are not looked upon as turf for development. How often have you heard, "He's such a natural in math, but he really needs work on his history and English"? Where is the emphasis? On history and English. But where is the greatest area for potential growth? In math.

Consider for a moment the issue of reading. The Nebraska School Study Council asked the University of Nebraska to launch a major three-year study to determine the most effective techniques for teaching speed reading. The study included more than one thousand students who were each tested for speed and comprehension. The results were dramatic. First of all, the best teachers got the best results, but the truly outstanding results were a product of the best teachers interacting with the best students. The poor readers, who started at 90 words per minute, made modest gains to an average of 150 words per minute. But the top readers, who started at 350 words per minute, multiplied to more than 2,900 words per minute! The results startled even the most experienced researchers, who assumed the poorest readers would make the greatest percentage gains.

The speediest readers grew the most and profited the most from more training.

MYTH #3: SUCCESS IS THE OPPOSITE OF FAILURE

The catch here is the belief that strengths are the opposite of weaknesses, illness is the opposite of health, success is the opposite of failure, good is the opposite of bad. They are not. Strengths and weaknesses, success and failure, good and bad, each has its own configuration, its own syndrome, its own pattern of behavior. Yet we are tricked into believing that if we find out what went wrong and fix it, everything will be right; if we identify our weaknesses, we can turn them into strengths. In fact, however, we cannot learn about strengths by studying and focusing on weaknesses.

Consider these situations:

1. Studying broken homes will not lead to information on building strong families.

2. Studying why young people use drugs will not lead us to an understanding of the conditions under which some children say no to drugs.

3. Studying why people leave companies will not tell managers why some people stay.

4. Studying why kids fail at math will not explain why some students excel.

The study of failure can give misleading clues about what to emphasize in improving performance. For instance, when the country is in an economic slump, economists and the media set about documenting the downturn from every angle. Corporate executives and sales managers begin to justify every problem in terms of the recession. Real though the inequities may be, focusing on weaknesses does not lead to progress. Only a study of why certain companies are successful during both recessions *and* boom times will offer tips for improvement. These companies no doubt move to the strengths of the marketplace. In any economic climate there is always opportunity for success.

MYTH #4: EVERYONE CAN DO ANYTHING THEY PUT THEIR MINDS TO

This myth takes many other forms:

> If at first you don't succeed, try, try again.
> Practice makes perfect.
> If you can conceive it, you can achieve it.
> If I can do it, you can do it.

These homilies are part of "the power of positive thinking" school, which suggests that success is simply a matter of hard work. While millions of ambitious and intelligent people today follow this deeply held American philosophy, many are destined for failure and frustration. The reason is fundamental. To theorize that "anyone can do anything" assumes that all people are clones, possessing an identical set of talents. This, of course, is false. We are each one of a kind, with a unique set of strengths. We are not robots able to be trained for anything with the right reinforcement. But while we know this from the research and writings of noted Harvard psychologist Dr. Gordon Allport and other respected researchers, the myth is pervasive and is shot through our popular media. The reality is that we can (and should) *try* anything we wish to try, but long-term success will elude us unless we determine early on that we have a basic talent for the endeavor. The phrases should read:

- You can be anything *your strengths* allow you to be.

- If at first you don't succeed, *check to see if you're building on a strength.*

- Practicing *a strength* makes perfect.

- If you can conceive it and achieve it, *it was probably there all along.*

- If I can do it, *those with the same strengths can too.*

Trying to succeed in an area in which you are weak will lead to a negative self-concept.

"Jan" is a thirty-year-old technical sales trainee for a copier manufacturer. After spending years in the support ranks, she decided to put her knowledge of the product to work in the sales arena where she had high hopes for success. But after six months, she was not first or second as she had expected, but fifteenth. She could talk the product and make fine presentations, but she lacked the courage to ask for the order. Prior to this disillusionment, she had been an inspiring member of the sales force, but her once-prominent leadership position faded as she became less self-assured. Failure soon spread to her personal life. By practicing a weakness, she was undermining her sense of self.

When we focus on a weakness, it takes on a life of its own and begins to smother our strengths. We start to feel sorry for someone's weakness and offer pity and philosophical advice. We try to comfort by saying: "If you think you've got it bad, just think how bad the poor sucker down the street has it." But focusing on failures will only make the person feel worse and neglect his or her strengths. The greatest chance for success lies in reminding people or organizations of an existing strength, and getting them back on track while instituting a management strategy for the weaknesses.

"Do not try to teach a pig to sing—it wastes your time and annoys the pig."

There is a cartoon of a pig with the caption, "Do not try to teach a pig to sing—it wastes your time and annoys the pig." This is terrific advice, and yet we try to teach pigs to sing in all levels of business and education. Each time we ask salespeople to become detail people who then struggle with call and expense reports; when managers with no interest in or inclination for selling are sent to sales courses; or when top engineers are promoted to management, we are trying to teach pigs to sing. We offer "singing lessons to pigs" in all levels of education where students are expected to excel in all subjects rather than encouraged and allowed to fulfill the basic requirements and focus on their area of strengths.

Focus on strengths and manage the weaknesses.

Could it be that the leaders and achievers in the new millennium will win the battle for excellence with a different set of weapons? We believe they will, and the strategy will be: Focus on strengths and manage the weaknesses.

CHAPTER 2

The Strengths' Theory: Focus on Strengths and Manage the Weaknesses

The Chinese have long held the Olympic gold medal in Ping-Pong. At the 1984 Olympics, when they again captured the gold, the coach of the Chinese team was asked by a reporter, "Tell us about your team's daily training regimen."

"We practice eight hours a day perfecting our strengths."

"Could you be a little more specific?"

"Here is our philosophy: If you develop your strengths to the maximum, the strength becomes so great it overwhelms the weaknesses. Our winning player, you see, plays only his forehand. Even though he cannot play backhand and his competition knows he cannot play backhand, his forehand is so invincible that it cannot be beaten."

This is the Strengths' Theory in a nutshell.

THE POWER OF
ONE SIMPLE QUESTION

"What would happen if we studied what was right with people versus what's wrong with people?" That simple question, posed by Don Clifton and his colleagues more than forty years ago while he was still a graduate student of educational psychology at the University of Nebraska, launched what we believe to be the most extensive research into positive behavior and success in history. Don was inspired by other thinkers, including Professor William E. Hall, who encouraged his students at the University of Nebraska to improve the mental health of people by studying and recognizing good behavior. Psychologists, he asserted, could have far greater impact if they studied people with good behavior rather than, as he put it, "the lame, the halt, and the lazy."

What was the benefit of studying what was right

with people? At a minimum, it would offer a whole new way of viewing the world.

Instead of thinking in terms of weaknesses, the focus would be on identifying and developing strengths while managing the weaknesses. For instance,

- Instead of zeroing in on what your child or your employees don't do well, the emphasis would be on helping them do more of what they are good at and managing their weak areas.

- Instead of focusing on fixing the federal deficit, the focus would be on developing the strengths of the economy *and* managing the federal deficit.

That one simple question triggered more than forty years of continuing research into the thoughts and behavior of successful people. To date, SRI Gallup, an international research and consulting firm dedicated to human resources research, has studied in depth more than 250,000 successful salespeople, managers, leaders, executives, teachers, doctors, pilots, and athletes. SRI Gallup research now stretches around the globe and includes studies at Federal Express; Marriott; Kentucky Fried Chicken; Golden Corral; Citicorp; Allied Lyons; Richman Gordman; Merck, Sharpe and Dohme; C. R. Bard; Springmaid; Canadian Pacific Hotels and Resorts;

General Motors; Volvo; Prudential Securities; British Airways; Alaska Airlines; Taco Bell; and hundreds more companies and over one thousand school districts across the United States.

This research led to three major conclusions:

1. The study of strengths creates a new theory of what people are like.

2. Maximum productivity can be gained by focusing on strengths and managing weaknesses.

3. The study of strengths leads to an understanding of the difference between good and great.

THE STUDY OF STRENGTHS CREATES A NEW THEORY OF WHAT PEOPLE ARE LIKE

Freud studied sick people and so developed his theories. The result? Today, most twelve-year-olds can spot the symptoms of depression, alcoholism, and neurosis. But can adults describe the strengths of their co-workers, families, and friends?

If we learned to spot strengths in ourselves, we would then know what to look for, what to develop,

recognize, and celebrate. That information won't come, however, from the traditional method of studying people—drawing a large sample and computing the mean performance for the group, then measuring individuals by how far they deviate from this average. That approach assumes that people have the same characteristics whether they are top performers or poor performers, that the best performers have the same qualities as the average performers, and that the only difference is degree. Our studies of success refute this.

- Great coaches are different from average coaches or even very good coaches in how they view winning. To the average coach, winning is defined as getting the better score. To the great coach, winning means doing things right, moving toward overall perfection.

- In a study of nurses, it was discovered that the best nurses need to use less medication with their patients because of their empathy with their patients.

- Outstanding managers have the capacity for seeing growth and development in their workers. It would be impossible to discover this in poor managers because they rarely notice such things.

- In a study of outstanding pilots, it was learned that the pilots who are most likely to survive a crisis are always thinking about backups. They like to set up practice crisis situations so that when a crisis does arise, they are ready to cope. During real crises, top pilots often experience déjà vu because they have already anticipated the situation!

- Exceptional salespeople have the courage to ask their customers to buy. Average or failing salespeople lack courage and often can't close. They offer new options, attempt to drop the price, and sell by making concessions.

- Outstanding workers feel a responsibility for their customers and so have a lower absentee rate. Poor workers are more focused on what they *don't* have to do.

- Prominent personnel officers in large companies have a unique capacity for empathizing with all the people in the company. Poor human resource professionals talk about compliance with company policy.

- Outstanding priests build caring relationships with their parishioners. Poor priests preach to their parishioners or rely on quotations from the scriptures.

- Great teachers show an ability to work with their students as equals, even in preschool. Poor teachers present information to be memorized.

THE STUDY OF STRENGTHS LEADS TO PRODUCTIVE CONCLUSIONS; THE STUDY OF WEAKNESSES LEADS TO INEFFECTIVE CONCLUSIONS

Dr. George Gallup, Sr., founder of the Gallup Organization, was another pioneer in the study of success. In the 1960s he studied 530 persons who had reached the age of ninety-five or older (193 were one hundred years of age or older). The survey interview, which asked over two hundred questions and took some three hours to complete, revealed insights that could never be learned by studying why people die early in life. For example, he discovered that those who live long were not "choosy" about their food or how it was prepared (a fact that would shock most modern dieticians), and many smoked and drank in moderation. The major discovery was that they were light eaters and weighed less than their peers, even during their forties and fifties. They ate less than the people with whom they lived—no snacks between meals, no bedtime snacks. Dr. Gallup suggested, "Perhaps the time has come to follow the custom of most countries and have only one substantial meal a day versus the routine of three square meals daily."

The study of success, however, is still the exception. Therefore, millions of decision makers are basing their decisions on misleading data.

For example, a study of a sample of teachers shows they have problems with discipline. So many administrators want to require these teachers to take additional courses in school discipline. Look what happens: The college courses on discipline encourage teachers to develop more rules and ultimately become more controlling, making them less effective in the classroom. On the other hand, we found that outstanding teachers spent time working on their relationships with the students. They thought about how they could help the students grow rather than how to control them, which inspired the students to cooperate.

In studies of ineffective leaders, it was found that they were reluctant to make decisions. The researchers concluded that good leaders make fast decisions. To help these leaders become more effective, they are offered courses on making fast decisions. But in our study of outstanding leaders, we found that their success was not because they made quick decisions. Instead, they displayed tolerance for ambiguity and could delay making decisions until all the facts were in.

The study of complaint letters can also lead corporate leaders in the wrong direction. A major auto manufacturer, eager to woo more of the women's market, called for an evaluation of all of the complaint letters from female customers. At the end of twelve months there was little or no increase in the number of female customers. It would have been better to look at the complimentary letters from female buyers.

Are we suggesting that only strengths should be emphasized and weaknesses be overlooked? No. The Strengths' Theory stresses that focus must be on strengths while weaknesses are to be managed, not ignored.

THE STUDY OF STRENGTHS LEADS TO AN UNDERSTANDING OF THE DIFFERENCE BETWEEN GOOD AND GREAT

The study of success has yet another dimension. It helps us differentiate between the very good and the great. A study reported in *Executive Newsline* prepared by the editors of *Psychology Today* states:

> One of the major differences between most long distance runners and world class marathoners is the way they handle physical pain during their long arduous races. Run of the mill runners disassociate (to cope with the pain). They, in effect, hypnotize themselves, cutting themselves off from their body's sensory feedback. Some people visualize their entire record collection, album by album, others run through their educational career as they race.

The article goes on to define the wall as the point at which a runner's will to continue begins to break down.

> However, world class runners are a different breed. Not only do they not disassociate, they dismiss the wall as unimportant. In the words of one such runner "the wall is a myth." The key is to read your body, adjust your pace, and avoid getting into trouble.

The best marathoners "associate" with the pain, constantly monitoring their body's signals. Instead of diverting their attention from their aching legs, they focus on them to remind themselves to stay loose and relax. Success has its own rules, and highly successful people look at the world in a different way. Too often our market studies institutionalize the behavior of the average rather than focusing on the most productive. Therefore, we cannot understand greatness by studying the average.

STUDY STRENGTHS: THE ROAD LESS TRAVELED

This deceptively simple-sounding theory has a ring of rightness to it. So why, you may ask, doesn't everyone follow it? Why aren't our companies set up so that the strong sellers sell and the people who are good with people manage? Why aren't our schools designed so that math aficionados pursue math, verbal whizzes pursue languages, and athletes pursue sports? Why don't politicians build on the strengths of our economy, and corporate leaders build on their best people, best products, and best divisions? In a handful of organizations, the theory is indeed at work.

On Wall Street: The Strengths
of Prudential Securities

Dolores Calcagno, vice president of training for Prudential Securities, is a spirited champion of the Strengths' Theory and has applied it to hiring and management practices. In the past, each of the 4,500 male and female account executives at Prudential Securities were all asked to do the same thing: work with existing customers and make cold calls to new prospects. Today, account executives are matched with their strengths. Some have spectacular success working with existing accounts while others relish the challenge of the cold call; they are all allowed to work according to their areas of competency.

Prudential Securities applied the theory to the area of risk tolerance. Their research found some account executives had a natural flair for high-risk options (on everything from stocks to silver and hog bellies) while others had spectacular results working day after day with clients on low-risk products including blue chips, annuities, and certificates of deposit. "Today, our focus is on the individual and his/her strengths. We don't ask guys who like to cold call to service existing accounts, or women who trade options to sell annuities." Dolores summarized her thoughts on the theory:

"If you don't focus on strengths today, you're playing a losing game."

_____

Individuals are always stronger when they have their successes and strengths clearly in mind.

_____

In the NFL: Developing Strengths

Vince Lombardi, the winner of two Super Bowl championships, applied the theory when he observed that after most football games were over, the errors were spotlighted instead of the successes. One day he proclaimed, "From now on, we only replay the winning plays." Look how the theory plays out. When are you most confident: when recalling a moment of success or a moment when you couldn't deliver the goods? *Individuals are always stronger when they have their successes and strengths clearly in mind.*

The Strengths' Theory:
A Mental Lens for Business

Fred Dobbs, president of the Dallas-based Dobbs Stanford, a $70-million electronics manufacturer's representative, found the Strengths' Theory "to be astonishingly right" and directly applicable to all stages of developing a business. "At first, when you're building a company, all you have time to do is flex your strengths . . . in our case that meant sell, sell, sell. But when the company matures, you begin to spend time thinking about making things right, and fixing your weaknesses." That's when you begin to lose your edge. "My partner and I even started a cold war over our obsession with each other's weaknesses. I wanted him to be more entrepreneurial like me, and he wanted me to be more like him—all organized, neat, and rational."

Dobbs now uses the theory as a "mental lens"—a way to view people based on who they are, based on their strengths instead of wasting time and resources on what they are not. He and his partner, Woody Taylor, credit the theory as responsible for getting them back on track.

A Freeing Experience:
Managing the Weaknesses

David Brown, a New York securities broker, has applied the theory in order to make a good situation even better. In 1989 his commissions topped the $500,000 mark, making him one of the top one percent of securities brokers in the nation. He reasoned that if he could devote 100 percent of his time to his primary strengths, that of working with customers, he could boost his commissions to $750,000 annually. To accomplish that goal, he applied the second portion of the theory: manage your weaknesses. He isolated his areas of weakness: specifically paperwork and reports, activities that chewed up more than 30 percent of his time. Brown adopted one of the four strategies we present in Chapter 4 for "managing the weaknesses" that freed him to exercise his strengths over the following twelve months and realize his goal in a rollercoaster stock market.

Rightness Versus Shoulds

Dana Jacobsen is a twenty-seven-year-old sales executive for a Denver consulting firm who told us how the Strengths' Theory allowed her to get back on her strength path. "I was a good, competent sales manager, but I knew from listening to other managers they were getting a different kick out of management than I was. After a few years I finally realized I needed to be the producer, not the manager of the producers. I loved getting on the phone, setting up meetings, making presentations, and getting the sale more than I valued hearing how someone else had done it. When I summoned up the courage to go back to direct selling, my friends and co-workers thought I was crazy. They all told me, 'Management is the way to the top, not direct sales.' "

In spite of the avalanche of peer pressure, Dana made the switch back to her area of strength, which not only netted her psychic rewards but financial and physical ones as well. "In my last few months as manager, I was taking eight to ten Tylenol a day. Now that I'm back to selling, the stress seems to have vanished."

Focus on Strengths by Weeding Out Weaknesses

David Marks is a Northern California entrepreneur who has built a ten-store specialty retail chain around the concept of name brands for low prices. Recently he observed that two of the stores were underperforming the top stores by 60 percent. So he went to work switching salespeople, working with the managers, and making store improvements. After four months and spending several hundred hours personally on this dilemma with only brief blips of improvement, he opted to close both stores and apply the same resources of time and money to his remaining eight stores.

Had Marks been from the school of "fix the weaknesses," he would still be attempting to bring the two stores up to the performance of the others. Instead he chose to discontinue the two operations, paying off the leases and moving the store managers to other stores. This surgery-type action was an act of courage few could match.

The Strengths' Theory Goes Home

Mark Abrahms, a manufacturing manager for a pharmaceutical company, found the Strengths' Theory so compelling that he walked out in the middle of a seminar to make a phone call. Later he told us, "I just had to call my son to praise him on his latest science project and apologize for hounding him for not going out for football. Here I was trying to make him well rounded and push him into football, and I was killing his strengths in science. It just struck me so clearly that focusing on my son's strengths was not only right, it was the loving thing to do."

THE SEARCH FOR STRENGTHS: A NEW DIRECTION

As you will discover, the Strengths' Theory applies on three different levels: as a *philosophy* for guiding your personal and professional life, as a *strategic tool* for decision making, and as a *system* for developing those around you. It is, above all, not just a clever-sounding bumper sticker slogan, but a proven strategy to increase productivity and performance.

Many people, intrigued by the theory, ask if we're promoting the development of strong people over those who are less talented and are, therefore, promoting an elitist concept. That would assume there are "less strong people." The Strengths' Theory is based on the premise that *every person can do one thing better than any other 10,000 people.*

Our goal, therefore, is to share our findings with everyone, from executives and managers, to students, educators, parents, and politicians, so that they can exercise their strengths and help others do the same. It is our hope that the trap of working blindly for the sake of working can be avoided.

That is the mission of this book—to help you recognize and use your strengths to achieve excellence. We all define ourselves through our work and accomplishments, and the more opportunities we have to know excellence, the more rewarded we will be.

As you read on you will come to understand the theory and the many ways it can be applied. You can use the theory to:

- Learn how to find out how good people can be by identifying their strengths rather than their weaknesses.

- Learn how to stop wasting time working on your weaknesses.

- Learn how to double and triple your productivity and effectiveness by exercising your strengths.

- Make dramatically more effective decisions by studying what's right versus what's wrong.

You will learn strategies to manage the things you don't do well and ways to identify and nurture the things you do best. We welcome you to join us on this marvelous journey we know can change the world . . . to a world built on the strengths of each of its inhabitants.

CHAPTER 3

Find Out What You Do Well and Do More of It

John Portman, the internationally acclaimed architect, celebrated for his work on the Renaissance Center in Detroit, the Peachtree Plaza, the Bonaventure, and the atriums concept in the Hyatt Hotels, was asked, "Can you remember when it was that you decided to become an architect?" He said he was in junior high school, when he took a course in mechanical drawing. The course so captured his imagination that he wanted to talk and think about drawing and sketching everywhere he went. At the time there were two high schools in Atlanta: one which focused on college prep, and one which offered many technical programs that would be helpful for his chosen field. With his future clearly in mind, he went to meet with the principal of the more technical school. Portman said, "Sir, I've taken this course in mechanical drawing. Now I know what I want to be. I want to be an architect." He continued, "I want to go to your school, but I only want to take the shop courses related to drawing and architecture and not all the rest." The principal said, "Young man, if at this age you have already decided what you want to do, I am not going to stand in your way."

Often, when people hear this story they say, "Oh, but John Portman won't be well rounded." What they really mean is he won't become a Renaissance man with all the refinements of Leonardo da Vinci, competent in literature, the arts, and science. How wrong.

A lot of knowledge about one subject offers the integrating point for all other knowledge.

Our studies of human development show that once a person has an area of competency, structuring of knowledge provides a framework for acquiring new knowledge and understanding. A lot of knowledge about one subject offers the integrating point for all other knowledge.

Strengths develop best when sufficient time is devoted to a single subject or goal. Once you are competent in a particular area, you can integrate other subjects. In this way, you can build on your experience. Leonardo's expertise in science and literature grew out of his priority strength, which was art; John Portman learned about the world from architecture; Armand Hammer grew from international business and art; Michael Jackson, on the other hand, organizes his life and learning around music.

Along with this insight comes the understanding that *not being everything is smart; not working on everything but rather emphasizing selected strengths is the route to excellence.* For many people, this understanding requires a redirection of the *doing all* and *being all* to *being more by focusing on less* and *doing a lot of what you do well.*

You can follow this advice by developing selected strengths and managing or dropping those activities and fantasies you pursue to no constructive end.

STRENGTHS: A DEFINITION

We define strengths on two different levels. On a rudimentary level, strengths are the things you do well.

Those strengths may include selling, developing the talents of others, shooting a basketball, giving a speech worthy of a standing ovation, being patient and understanding with second graders, or having a green thumb.

On a more sophisticated level, a strength is a pattern of behavior, thoughts, and feelings that produces a high degree of satisfaction and pride; generates both psychic and/or financial reward; and presents measurable progress toward excellence.

Notice the key words in this latter definition: behavior, thoughts, and feelings. We do not limit this definition to having a specific skill but enlarge it to encompass motives and drives. While physical skills are one form of strength, the second type has more to do with motivations such as ego, persistence, dedication, courage, pride, perfection, and competition. Interestingly, motivations often function as the driving force of success. Did Andy Warhol become a world-famous artist because of his artistic talent or because of his need to define himself as a significant human being? Did Winston Churchill become the voice of Britain and prime minister because of his leadership capabilities or because of his enormous courage and his drive to become a significant human being? The answer could be either or both.

THE FIVE CHARACTERISTICS
OF A STRENGTH

When shaping and building an organization or your own personal future, unearthing your own strengths, and those of others, is one of the most valuable discoveries any leader can make. Here you will learn the five characteristics of a strength and then critical steps for developing strengths. The following characteristics are designed to help you scan your life for anything you have ever done well. Don't restrict yourself to current strengths. Strengths can be drawn from childhood, college, or the present day. While scanning for strengths, be sure you look within yourself.

One: Listen for Yearnings

Strengths start first in the mind of the performer, so that is where we will begin. Yearnings are part of the wisdom of the body. They can be characterized as the pull or attraction to one activity over another. Yearnings are most often triggered when you see a performance or someone performing an activity and you say to yourself, "I'd like to do that; I'd like to try that."

Like an internal magnet, yearnings pull us toward one thing instead of another, a process that begins in early childhood. It is yearnings that influence us to build a tree house, set up a lemonade stand, or rig an Apple computer to communicate with hackers around the country. Often those early yearnings are so powerful, they chart the course of one's lifework. Bruce Hangen, conductor of the Omaha Symphony Orchestra, tells about his experience in junior high school: "Just sitting there in my position as first cellist, I knew I wanted to get up and lead the orchestra, and I knew I could do it better than my teacher." One day he summoned the courage to ask the orchestra director if he could lead the orchestra. The director said, "Of course," handed him the baton, and his career was launched.

Of course, "yearning" to do something doesn't end when you become an adult. In a recent Gallup poll, we found that for 65 percent of the adults polled, "starting their own company" was a significant desire. Of those polled, a full 35 percent expected to act on that yearning within the coming twenty-four months.

Like the more than 750,000 female entrepreneurs in the United States, Lane Nemeth yearned to do her own thing. In 1972, while working as a teacher in a day care center, it struck her how few toys were available to parents that were designed as educational tools. Sensing the need, she proceeded to scrape up $25,000 in backing, began negotiations with manufacturers all over the world, and launched Discovery Toys, a company that distributes educational products through more than 20,000 independent distributors in the United States, Canada, and Japan.

Listening for the Yearnings in Others: A Leaders' Tool

Leaders who listen to the yearnings of their people use them as a clue to identifying strengths. One CEO of a computer distribution firm in Chicago reported to us how he applied this insight to recruiting a new purchasing manager for one of his divisions. "On a flight to Chicago, I began jotting down the 'yearnings' of my top management group." High on his list was a district sales manager who had repeatedly expressed interest in heading up purchasing. Until then, his response had been to humor him, while soberly thinking "Why risk a change and potentially lose a good manager?" But he took to heart the value of yearnings as a predictor of strengths. When an opening in purchasing did come, he offered him the spot. "Now that he's taken the reins, he's proven to be the most successful purchasing manager we've ever had."

Misleading Yearnings

The mere existence of a yearning is not the sine qua non of a strength, but it does offer the first concrete clue to the existence of one. For example, how many people do you know who yearn to be a manager for the sake of *power,* to be one step closer to the corner office, the corporate jet, or the golden parachute? In reality, they show little concern for the primary mission of management: the development of people. We term this a *misyearning*—one that can derail us from our strengths' path.

Glamour and excitement are two more hooks that can trigger a misyearning. Recently we completed a study of flight attendants for one of the major airlines. We found those attendants with poor performance and poor retention (less than eighteen months) tended to focus on the glamour and excitement of jetting from city to city, meeting fascinating people, and getting low-cost tickets to exotic foreign ports instead of the real-world experience of dealing with tired travelers, spending repeated nights on the road, and serving thousands of snacks and meals. The "best" flight attendants, our study showed, were obsessed with making people comfortable. Their primary mission was customer service, not glamour.

Misyearnings can also be motivated by the "friendly advice of others" or even "lucrative job offers" that sound appealing and may be financially rewarding but ultimately land us on the wrong track. It's easy to get trapped by what others think while ignoring our real strengths.

Two: Watch for Satisfactions

Jeff Smith, the best-selling cookbook author and television personality, The Frugal Gourmet, oozes with a sense of satisfaction over every dish he concocts and every food fact he has a chance to communicate.

Joe Montana, quarterback of the San Francisco 49ers, talks of experiencing a similar sense of satisfaction when he completes a perfect pass, while leaders like Lee Iacocca and Norman Schwarzkopf reflect a kind of arrogant satisfaction in their ability to lead brilliantly under the most challenging of circumstances.

Satisfactions are those experiences where the emotional and psychic rewards are great; typically they are the activities we get "a kick out of doing." Satisfactions are not merely momentary pleasures, but form our intrinsic motivation. The pleasure sensation that is created each time we perform a particular task forms the internal or psychological motivation to repeat an activity time and again.

Satisfactions, like yearnings, are rarely present where basic strengths are not. In the movie *Broadcast News*, there is a scene where the investigative reporter finally gets his chance to anchor the news, which he had politicked for since his first days in television. But his dream turns to pure horror when once in the anchor chair, talking straight to camera, he begins to sweat profusely. Perspiration cascades off his face onto his clothes and copy. Viewers, so disturbed by this sight, jammed the station switchboard to ask if he was having a heart attack. Even this cocky, ego-laden character knew the truth when he experienced it. Instead of a satisfying experience, it was one he never wanted to repeat. Contrast this with the star of the movie, the not-too-bright anchor, played by William Hurt. For him, anchoring was an experience of total satisfaction even though "he often didn't know what he was talking about."

Competencies and satisfactions are not always

partners. Recently a successful Wall Street type asked us: "I make six figures a year, I'm terrific at what I do, and I hate it. Is that a strength?" No. Most competencies that aren't satisfying are short lived, lasting only until something more interesting comes along. While our Wall Street friend may be good at what he does (internal auditing for a major brokerage firm), odds are he will burn out owing to his lack of satisfaction. Our message: If it doesn't feel good, you are not practicing a strength.

Three: Watch for Rapid Learning

If you catch on quickly to something, you're likely to be good at it. The dominant feeling with rapid learning is "I feel like I've always known how to do this."

Think of your own experiences: learning a new computer program, assembling patio furniture, or feeling ready to sell a product the first day of a training program. In each instance, you either caught on quickly, slowly, or not at all.

In sales, for instance, we divide top salespeople into two categories: the naturals and the competents. Both can be rapid learners. While the competents may learn rapidly in traditional ways with textbooks and three-ring binders, natural salespeople do not want "experts" around unless they ask for them, which results in these natural salespeople wanting to "go it alone" early in the game. The naturals are those who learn by "jumping in"—they would prefer to go out on a call to learn the process rather than sit through a training course. Their rapid learning occurs not from a textbook or a three-ring binder, but from hearing the customers ask questions and then formulating the answers. Interestingly, new recruits who are naturals in selling value the product highly and are able to build trust rapidly. Those strengths allow them to get a jump start over the run-of-the-mill salespeople.

Slow Learning: He Just Doesn't Get It

Slow learning is evidence of a nonstrength and takes place at every level of an organization, including the board of directors. The head coach of a New England college football team told us of his moments at a board meeting:

"At our last annual meeting, the financial statements were passed out to each of us and the comptroller proceeded to review the highlights. It was embarrassing because I asked questions again and again. He explained, but I just didn't get some of that financial stuff. I know about sales, but I feel brain dead with finance." For our friend, the annual meeting wasn't a moment of rapid learning, and it isn't ever likely to be. His strengths lie in another area.

_____

**A strength is always
characterized by initial rapid
learning, learning that continues
throughout one's lifetime.**

_____

Slow learning isn't a factor to be dismissed lightly. It's so significant as an indicator of a nonexistent strength that it can never be discounted on the assumption that a person will "get it someday." Do you know someone who:

- Reads and rereads legal documents to no avail?

- Attempts to read maps and blueprints with barely an ounce of understanding?

- Regularly attends football games and never learns the plays?

- Repeatedly hurts others' feelings even after years of counseling?

A strength is always characterized by initial rapid learning, learning that continues throughout one's lifetime.

Four: Glimpses of Excellence

You can spot a strength by glimpsing a moment of excellence within a performance. When we speak of a performance, we are referring to a finite activity: the singing of a song, the writing of a letter, the presenting of a speech, the greeting of people at a function, the tallying of a hotel bill, the servicing of a customer in a restaurant. A performance is made up of a series of "moments" that can offer clues to a strength.

The story of a Midwest high school track coach illustrates this point. Bob Timmons, a coach in Topeka, Kansas, tells of a day when he was at the track watching the new sophomore recruits run three laps around the field. He thought to himself, "What a bunch of ugly ducklings." Six months later, he spent the afternoon, with stopwatch in hand, timing each of the remaining runners.

As he was glancing back and forth between his stopwatch and a presumed "ugly duckling," he did a double take. "The boy ran his first lap in 64.8, his second in 68.7, and his third in 69.6. He certainly had improved since September." All at once, it struck him,

"That's no ugly duckling. He's become a beautiful swan."

After the workout, he called the runner over and said, "Son, you've got a chance to run the mile in under four minutes in high school."

The young man responded, "Coach, you're crazy."

But the coach was certain it was possible since he had seen a nearly identical pattern in another track star he had coached earlier.

On March 29, 1966, Jim Ryan proved Coach Timmons right. He ran the mile in 3.51 minutes, becoming the world's fastest man.

Only the trained eye can glimpse moments of excellence. Coaches like Timmons are able to spot the more subtle critical moments in runners. A top sales manager is able to glimpse a moment of excellence in a salesperson when he or she can clearly and directly ask for the order, zero in on the need and thoughts of the customer and ask exactly the right question, or exhibit perfect timing by knowing the right moment during the sale to ask: "Can we sign this now?"

One of the most effective ways to master this technique is by studying success. Only when you know what success looks like can you see its subtleties. For example, only when you study a Rolls-Royce up close can you know what its hood ornament looks like. Notice the people around you: your associates, co-workers, and directors. Watch them when they are at the peak of their performance. Notice how the chairman makes a decision and directs the company, the way your receptionist makes people feel very special, or how your top salesperson pauses dramatically while the prospect reaches for a pen. The more you study success, the more you will begin to see it. Along with that special insight comes the responsibility: to applaud those "glimpses" in others as often as possible.

Five: Total Performance of Excellence

On February 26, 1990, Paula Zahn stepped into the lives of approximately 3 million viewers when she took over as co-anchor of *CBS This Morning*. The newspaper reviews the following day nearly all mirrored this headline: "Zahn didn't miss a beat." From the moment the second hand touched 7:00 A.M. to 120 minutes later, Zahn showed her CBS colleagues and the viewers across America a level of competence not often seen on the first day of a show. It was a perfect example of total performance.

Total performance of excellence is a flow of behavior, when there are no conscious steps in the mind of the performer. Studies we have conducted of the best basketball players tell us when they do a slam dunk or another of their very best plays, they act almost unconsciously. They are on automatic, at one with the activity. The clock doesn't tick.

Total performance comes when you're writing a report and the words begin to flow together, or when you make a follow-up sales call and your message comes out clear and convincing. It may happen when you're heading a meeting and the energy in the room increases as you speak, and you know you're motivating your people. It may be as subtle as conversing with a friend and noticing she is listening to you raptly. It occurs when priests share the perfect homily with a person in emotional pain, or when nurses give painless injections.

Total performance isn't a glimpse but the complete extension of an activity. It doesn't happen occasionally, but each time the activity is performed. It is not subject to circumstances but transcends them.

News anchor Connie Chung is a case in point. She began her career in Washington, D.C., at CBS and then moved to a co-anchor position at a CBS station in Los Angeles. Eight years later she again moved up, to the evening news in New York. Her broadcast strengths were not limited but grew and adapted to new audiences in major cities.

Total performance of excellence is the ultimate indication of a strength. It's the quality that managers, leaders, and parents try to build upon. When total performance occurs in children, it need not evolve into their lifework. For instance, when a child throws a ball like a pro or shows gymnastic talent, these moments of total performance can develop the child's self-esteem, which will help the youngster in other endeavors.

One final test of total performance is the improvement of an activity over a period of time. The satisfaction gained through total performance will cause a person to want to repeat it, but with the repetition must come improvement. For a salesperson this means measurable increases in sales. For the manager it is measured by the improved performance of his or her people.

Strengths Versus Advantages

A strength is an inner ability, something that can be displayed in a performance, versus a material possession or a title.

For instance, a Harvard MBA is an advantage but not a strength. It provides knowledge and often functions as a door opener. But an advantage can only get you in the door for an interview or a meeting; a strength is required to convert the advantage into a beneficial result. A million-dollar inheritance is an advantage, but the ability to build on (and not lose) an inheritance is a strength.

The ability to separate personal strengths from advantages is vital. If you don't separate them, you may end up spending wasted time on the wrong things. To help you, we have devised the following quiz.

Is it a strength or an advantage to:

Strength   Advantage

1. Have a new car
2. Belong to a golf club
3. Have an MBA
4. Author a best seller
5. Have imagination
6. Have a great family
7. Run the marathon
8. Be president of a company
9. Have a sense of humor
10. Be able to judge character
11. Write poetry
12. Fly a plane
13. Lead and motivate people

14. Be a U.S. Senator
15. Have lots of friends
16. Be a manager or executive
17. Be friendly
18. Know how to make money
19. Program a computer
20. Be competitive
21. Be courageous
22. Have a beautiful home
23. Be a good salesperson
24. Be able to organize people*

PICK ONE STRENGTH AND PURSUE IT

Luciano Pavarotti, the superstar tenor, tells of the time in his life when he had to sort his strengths.

"When I was a boy, my father, a baker, introduced

* ANSWERS: 1. Advantage, 2. Advantage, 3. Advantage, 4. Strength, 5. Strength, 6. Advantage, 7. Strength, 8. Advantage, 9. Strength, 10. Strength, 11. Strength, 12. Strength, 13. Strength, 14. Advantage, 15. Advantage, 16. Advantage, 17. Strength, 18. Strength, 19. Strength, 20. Strength, 21. Strength, 22. Advantage, 23. Strength, 24. Strength.

me to the wonders of song. He urged me to work very hard to develop my voice. Arrigo Pola, a professional tenor in my hometown of Modena, Italy, took me as a pupil. I also enrolled in a teachers' college. On graduating, I asked my father, 'Shall I be a teacher or a singer?'

" 'Luciano,' my father replied, 'if you try to sit on two chairs, you will fall between them. For Life, you must choose one chair.' "

And so it is with strengths.

How do you know which strength to pursue? Multiple strengths are a common dilemma. We call it the smart person's disease—either you are good at a number of things or you feel that being good at a number of things is what winners do.

Cary Ross is a successful Beverly Hills attorney blessed with multiple talents including the ability to win cases, negotiate deals, manage his father's successful multimillion-dollar real estate development company, and function as the head of a monument company that erects customized sculptures for cities and municipalities. His strengths are tenacity, courage, competitiveness, and charm. But as Pavarotti's father said, you must pick one chair. At best, with his current schedule, Cary can expect to be average in all areas. By his own account, "I have become a jack-of-all-trades and master of none." Being a jack-of-all-trades or a Renaissance man is very much in vogue. It is often praised and thought to be the province of smart people. People pursuing multiple strengths are thought to be talented jugglers, like those on the *Ed Sullivan Show* who kept ten or twelve plates whirling at the same time. It makes for an interesting bit of entertainment, but it will net you mediocrity in the long run.

In 1921 Dr. Louis B. Terman, a Stanford University psychologist, set about the study of genius by tracking 1,470 genius-level children throughout their lifetime. The study was known as "the granddaddy of all life-span research." When Terman retired, the research was transferred to Drs. Robert and Pauline Sears. The data showed that exceptional intelligence does not guarantee extraordinary accomplishment. According to the study, what distinguished those of spectacular achievement from those of low achievement and failure was "prudence and forethought, willpower, perseverance and desire. They chose among their many talents and concentrated their efforts."

It may sound charming that young Mary or Tom is active in a dozen different activities, but it is the child who develops an area of talent and perfects it who excels, not the dilettante.

CLAIMING YOUR STRENGTH PATH: OUT OF FANTASY, INTO ACTION

It may take a while to sort your strengths because invariably you will have to let go of one activity or another that you dearly love. But when the decision is made, you will go for your goal no matter what. All at once, your questions and doubts are gone, and the path is cleared to move forward. This decisiveness nearly always follows a time of musing, tossing around the pros and cons. But soon you will be the manager, go for the promotion, try out for the play, or launch a company. You will often feel fear, but fear with an interesting quality to it. It's the moment, for instance, when you choose to pursue an MBA or a law degree, and the gnawing questions of "Will I stick it out? Will I embarrass the family? Will I flunk out?" fade away to be replaced with the power of clarity and determination. It's the moment when you've accepted the risks and push on in spite of them. It's the moment that fear, while still existing, is superceded by the excitement of your new commitment—when you strike a direction and "go for it."

ANY STRENGTH WORTH PURSUING IS WORTH PURSUING TO EXCESS

Clint Black, the country music singer and winner of the 1990 Grammy Award for Best Country Singer of the Year, always knew he was a singer even while working as an iron worker. But he didn't take his future for granted. Instead, he actively pursued every opportunity to ply his strength—singing in clubs, on porches, and at every church gathering—knowing full well that these occasions would lead to improvement and getting discovered.

And so it is for every field of endeavor.

It is not enough to have the strength for leadership without developing it.

It is not enough to have the strength to write, to communicate with the written word, without sitting down and practicing the craft.

But so often we follow the knee-jerk reaction: Once we learn what our strengths are, we quickly get to work on our weaknesses, because we honestly feel that's the route to success.

It's an honest assumption, but it will not net the desired results.

The Achievement of Mastery

In his book *Teaching and Learning Conditions for Extreme Levels of Talent Development,* Dr. Benjamin Bloom of Northwestern University in 1982 reported a study to determine the time it takes to achieve world-class competency in a field. The study, called the Development of Talent Project, analyzed the careers of world-class concert pianists, sculptors, research mathematicians, research neurologists, Olympic swimmers, and tennis champions.

The study found the answer to be between ten and seventeen years. For example, in a study of the winners of the Chopin International Piano Competition, the Tchaikovsky International Competition, and the Van Cliburn International Quadrennial Piano Competition, the ultimate competitive forums for pianists, it was found that pianists worked 17.14 years from the day they began taking piano lessons to the day they won a major competition.

So when you find out what you do well, do a *lot* of it. You must totally commit to one strength, being careful not to spread yourself thin. You must try not to let your other strengths distract you.

DO MORE OF IT: PRACTICING A STRENGTH MAKES PERFECT

Practice is the classic activity of successful people even at their peak. Curtis Strange, the PGA winner and national champion, begins each season by hitting two thousand golf balls a day in preparation for the tour.

Sidney Sheldon, the best-selling novelist, approaches writing by turning out fifty pages a day and not missing a day. (The average goal for a writer is four pages.)

And so it is for pilots, surgeons, managers, leaders, teachers. Excellence is developed by repeating a strength.

World-class managers we have studied tell how they spend their time: They spend time with their people, they tell anecdotes about them, they are their advocates. They like arranging and planning events for them; they are constantly encouraging them.

World-class pilots like to talk about flying. They are always considering the "what-ifs," from how to handle rough weather to what to do if a mechanical failure occurs. These pros are able to perform miracles, like the airliner that landed in Hawaii after the skin of the plane had blown off. These pilots had spent considerable time in flight simulators and in the actual seat, flying. So when the time of crisis came, they performed magnificently, as if they had been there before.

ENJOY IT: RELIVE YOUR SUCCESS

Enjoying your success is a tough assignment since we're so used to inspecting weaknesses versus showcasing strengths. But we are asking you to relive your success, to enjoy it over and over again. The more times you think of yourself doing your very best work, the more you are inviting success in the future. Remember: People or organizations are never stronger than when they have their successes clearly in mind. We suggest three steps for achieving this strength: visualize, write, and talk.

Picture It

Visualization is the process by which we mentally rehearse. Consider how a baseball pitcher might use this tool. Over and over again, the pitcher pictures himself walking out to the mound, spotting the catcher's cues, going through the windup, and making the pitch. This mental rehearsal allows the pitcher to relive all the emotions and satisfactions of the moment. Each time those satisfying feelings are recalled, the pitcher feels inspired and wants to further develop his strengths.

But visualization can backfire. When applied to a weakness, visualization becomes useless since no amount of imagery can turn a weakness into a strength. These are visualizations not of strengths but of "I wannas." This is regularly played out in Hollywood with actors and actresses who are always trying but never seem to get the part. Without the requisite strength, visualization will rarely get them beyond the casting call.

Write About It

Write down a full description, characterizing the strength: where it takes place, what it feels like when you're practicing it, your greatest moment experiencing it. Pack in all the imagery you can, for the more vivid the description, the more likely it is that the strength will recur.

Here are the transcribed, edited notes of a former insurance executive exploring a new career as a professional speaker:

> When I'm giving a speech, it makes me feel powerful; I love sharing information with people, making

them laugh, even making them cry (I can do that, you know). When I'm at the podium, I feel in total control. Sometimes I feel like a lion tamer at the circus—getting the audience to respond on cue. But I'm never sure.

I love the buildup to the talk, the fear of not being good enough. That pushes me to work on getting the speech better and better. I write out my entire speech in longhand early in the morning before my talks so it's fresh. But there's always an element of uncertainty in every talk. There's the challenge of winning them over (even though rationally I know I can't get every one of them to love me or even respect me). I go for respect.

Talk About It

Talk about what it feels like when you are exercising your strengths, what your proudest moments are when using them. Talk about the people who are tops in your field whom you would like to emulate and how you compare with them.

STAYING ON YOUR STRENGTHS' PATH

"What should I be doing right now?" That's a question you, Gloria Steinem, or President Bush can ask at any given moment, and you'll find this answer: Find out what you do well and do more of it. It is a message that will bring you back to your strengths' track, a track from which you can easily derail. Fans and detractors alike talk of how Donald Trump went off track at the height of his success because he became distracted by the media attention. Instead of focusing on his deal-making strengths, he became a media star. Heady stuff, but potentially disastrous. But doesn't the same thing happen to most people when they experience a little success, when they get their first promotion? We have a theory: The more successful a person gets, the greater the odds of falling off the strengths' path. Think back to the most famous failures of the eighties . . .

- The Wall Street brains who abused their strengths in the pursuit of greed.

- The sports star who started making movies.

- The retailing magnate who pulled off a leveraged buyout only to topple a host of quality department stores in quick succession (and declare bankruptcy) in the next twenty-four months.

In each case, they lost sight of the value of exercising the strengths that had brought them to the pinnacle.

The moral: The most precious and coveted perks can disappear or become meaningless if the critical strengths are not continually engaged. As recent history shows us, when strengths are not exercised or when they are abused, the fall from grace is swift.

CHAPTER 4

Find Out What You Don't Do Well and Stop Doing It

Stephen J. Cannell is one of Hollywood's most prolific television writers and producers. Since his studio was founded in 1980, it has produced two dozen prime-time series with 350 episodes, including *The A Team, Hunter,* and *Wiseguy.* Emmy Award–winning Cannell is also responsible for the *Rockford Files* and *Baretta.* Writing is clearly his strength. His weakness is dyslexia, a condition that causes him to transpose numbers and letters. Instead of trying to get over it or become an ace reader, he accepts what he doesn't do well and manages it. "It's something you cannot get over. I'm bad at spelling and sequencing and all the things that gave me trouble in high school. I'm as bad today as I was then." To manage his dyslexia, he dictates his material to his longtime assistant.

When we speak of weaknesses, we do not mean *everything* you don't do well, only what intrudes on your areas of productivity or lessens your self-esteem. In this chapter we want to think about your life and the areas that might be hampered by a weakness. Think about tasks such as paperwork; activities such as meetings; skills such as reading and writing; the larger arena of relationships with co-workers; and the possibility of substance abuse.

When you unearth a weakness, you must manage it and never think that it can be turned into a strength. True, some apparent weaknesses can be corrected with an extraordinary amount of time, energy, and money, but there is no alchemy for weaknesses. They can be removed but they cannot be transformed into strengths. The goal, therefore, is to manage weaknesses so the strengths can be freed to develop and become so powerful they make the weaknesses irrelevant.

That dictum is a tall order since it's downright heroic to work diligently on that which we don't do well. We estimate that for every one strength in our repertoire, we possess roughly one thousand nonstrengths. That ratio shows it would be a huge waste of energy to try to fix all of our weaknesses.

There is no alchemy for
weaknesses. They can be
removed but they cannot be
transformed into strengths.
The goal, therefore, is to manage
weaknesses so the strengths can
be freed to develop and become
so powerful they make the
weaknesses irrelevant.

Nevertheless, it's our culture's instinct to fix them, and so the idea of *managing* one's weaknesses, versus fixing them, is the most challenging part of the Strengths' Theory.

Recently we talked with a computer salesperson we'll call Joan who has the potential to be a top producer. We asked her how she used her time. "I'm real organized. From 8:00 A.M. to noon I make calls following up with clients, scheduling demonstrations and meetings for the following week, and I use the afternoon to meet with clients and prospective clients." When we asked her how she handled her paperwork, she visibly flinched. "Every time I see a form—a call report, expense report, even my checkbook register, I get uptight. What really makes me crazy is that I belong to Mensa, have an I.Q. of 146, and I still can't handle these blasted reports. Like clockwork, my manager always calls when he hasn't gotten any reports and makes me feel guilty. So I clear away some selling time (which infuriates me since I sell on commission) and force myself to fill out those damn little boxes."

Consider what Joan could produce if she managed her paperwork by hiring someone to write up the reports and devoted all of her time to selling. Could she increase her sales by 30 percent if she knew she would never have to face another call or expense report ever again? Our research indicates that she could. But *as long as she continues to tackle chores that she doesn't do well, she will be controlled by her weaknesses while her strengths limp along. Only at the moment when she starts to manage her weaknesses will she be in control of them.*

Do we mean that you shouldn't even try to work on areas of weakness? Of course not. We think that you should work on them as long as you like; but at some point you will have to decide whether your efforts are getting you anywhere. If the answer is "not far," then you should stop and apply the same energy to a strength.

Most weaknesses can't and don't need to be corrected any more than a doctor needs to repair an enlarged appendix. The patient needs only one thing—swift action to remove the weakness. Without the appendix, the patient can lead a healthy life.

That medical metaphor is the object lesson of this chapter.

You will find here no prescriptions for fixing weaknesses, no suggestions to attend courses or keep a journal. Instead you will find a way to build strengths by managing your weaknesses—an admittedly tough task, but necessary.

This philosophy is elegantly and powerfully stated in the famous Serenity Prayer:

> God grant me the power to accept
> the things I cannot change,
> the courage to change the things that I can,
> and the wisdom to know the difference.

In reality, this prayer is the embodiment of our theory. Weaknesses are the things that cannot be changed; strengths are the things that can be. (This process is also the basis of Alcoholics Anonymous and the other Anonymous programs where the goal is to manage the weaknesses, whether they are drugs, alcohol, or food, in order to clear the path for strengths.)

THE EIGHT STEPS TO IDENTIFYING WEAKNESSES

While the flaws in the examples we have presented so far may seem patently clear, identifying your own weaknesses (or those of your organization, associates, friends, or family members) may not be that easy. To help you along, we have singled out the eight behavioral clues that might indicate a weakness.

I. Feel Defensive About Performance

When a person is functioning in an area of weakness and, therefore, not performing up to his or her capability, be prepared for a barrage of defensive statements and behavior. Some examples are:

A. If I were younger, I'd be able to sell twice as much.

B. I'm just trying to catch up. If I had the same background as you, I'd be able to run those meetings, too.

C. You get all the breaks because you guys stick together.

This defensive behavior is everywhere:

- Sales managers with little discrimination blame their low sales on what the salespeople didn't do.

- Teachers weak in teaching skills pin the blame on the students.

- Profitless CEOs blame their lackluster bottom line on the economy.

- Parents blame their child's delinquency on the school.

- Poor salespeople blame their low sales figures on the lack of backup.

Individuals who are functioning in their area of strength show little or no defensive behavior. They meet challenges such as a downturn in the economy with a doubling of activity, and progress is the norm, not the exception.

2. Develop Obsessive Behavior

Often we obsess over weaknesses in our attempts to correct them. A kind of negative addiction takes over, and the strengths we would normally use in pursuing our talents go to work bolstering whatever we don't do well. One of our associates tells of her heroic and traumatic experience in trying to learn how to ski. For seven years she worked at mastering the stem christie and the most rudimentary moves on the slopes. She subscribed to skiing magazines, joined skiing clubs, and kept up on the latest ski fashions and trends. She only became more fearful. But instead of giving up (and moving on to tennis, an area of strength), she augmented her ski trips with Librium three times a day, to cope with her fear of the lifts and her stark terror of skiing down the runs. Her fear reached its peak one day. "I got on the advanced slope by mistake and was so overcome I took off my skis and spent the next ninety minutes walking down the three-mile run to the lodge." But the experience didn't stop her or even give her pause. She just kept on redoubling her efforts. But even the tranquilizers couldn't mask her sense of failure at the lodge where everyone bragged about their "great runs." For this highly competitive psychologist, the experience was ego crushing.

Why did she continue for seven years? She had become addicted to trying to master a weakness, and the addiction was fueled by her strengths: her competitiveness and her tenacity. She was from the school that said she could achieve anything she set her mind to. Not until she recognized her skiing forays for what they were could she let go of her obsession and switch over to the ego-enhancing game of tennis. (From our studies of highly competitive people, we know they need to be in situations where they can win on a predictable basis.)

Contrast that woman's addictive behavior with someone who pursues a talent and finds that with time he or she measurably improves. In psychology, that experience is called the learning curve. In the case of "naturals," dramatic leaps of understanding will take place. (When that happens, the best move then is to get out of the person's way!)

3. Experience Slow Learning

Corporate training classes are fertile territory for slow learning. A handful of new employees can always be found working on the same questions on the fourth day of the seminar as they were on the first. We see it again in boardrooms where executives are riffling through financial statements in a controlled but desperate attempt to decipher the numbers and ratios. Both are waltzing to rap music. Nothing clicks. There are no "ah-has," not only on the first try but after many attempts.

Even with these clues, the quest for mastery continues, sacrificing both time and money. How many Wall Street investors continually break even or claim losses because they just don't understand the dynamics of the market or the rhythm of Wall Street? Yet they stay in the game, talking the language of the street and keeping close tabs on the indicators.

4. Don't Profit from Repeated Experience

We see this no-growth behavior in tenured professors at universities who in their twentieth year of teaching use the same notes and anecdotes they used in their first year. We see stagnant growth in:

- Salespeople who consistently come in at the bottom of overall performance because they "visit" versus sell.

- Bankers who make too many shaky loans year after year.

- Golfers whose scores drop from 110 to 106 after playing eighteen holes twice a week for ten years.

- Sales managers whose sales remain flat year after year.

This phenomena contrasts with slow learning in that these people "get" an activity just enough to be functional, just enough to "hang in there," but lack the basic talent to achieve excellence. We even have a name for them—plodders. Their singular talent is not skill but tenacity and the fact that they always show up. (Unfortunately, some upper-level managers actively participate in this conspiracy by retaining plodders because they are easier to manage and control, and many are promoted to management.) By practicing a strength, you will always grow. If you exercise a weakness, your efforts will feel like molasses in January.

5. Consciously Think Through the Steps of a Process

In the early stages of learning any activity, whether it is programming a computer, learning a typewriter keyboard, the steps of a sale, or the elements of a speech, processing the steps in your mind is normal.

Contrast this with a situation in which no conscious step-by-step thought is required. For those who have a talent for a particular activity, the steps disappear very early, quickly fading as the subconscious takes over. But for someone with less talent, the steps always remain. Does Michael Jordan think through the steps to making a slam dunk? Of course not. The action is unconscious and automatic. There is a flow. The same is true of the finest managers. They don't think through the process of relating to or developing people. They act. For those without talent in a particular area, the steps always remain. The dance steps continue to flash in one's mind while on the dance floor, and the lips of a poor reader continue to sound out words decades after graduation from high school. The persistence of the steps indicates a weakness, one that could be cannibalizing strengths.

6. Experience a Reduction in Confidence from Performing the Activity

In each of the examples we have profiled in this chapter there is a psychological price tag: a reduction of self-esteem. For example, a highly motivated salesperson who never achieves any major breakthroughs will often display the following:

- A loss of interest and motivation.

- An increase in sick days.

- Mounting excuses for poor performance.

7. Lack Futuristic Thinking About the Activity

When practicing a weakness, you just want to get through it. When thinking about what you can't do, the only time is now. Whatever you are doing consumes all of your energies, leaving you precious little for thoughts of the future. However, when thinking about what you can do, you have a vision of the future. You have an idea of where your talents will lead you.

8. Suffer Burnout While Practicing an Activity

Experts often justify and explain burnout by clichés such as "all work is stressful" or "we live in a stress-filled society." But both statements are misleading. Burnout is often the mental and physical result of working in an area of weakness; it is final proof that the weakness exists.

Burnout is produced by the resistance you experience when doing what you're not good at. The resistance may be manageable in the early stages, but over time it accumulates until you reach a breaking point when you say to yourself, "I can't do this anymore." Burnout often spills over into other parts of your life. We call this the Spread of Effect when failure in one area is so profound it has a ripple effect on your personal life, children, family, and friends. Actions become efforts. Deeds become debilitating.

A person with a strength for accounting can enter numbers into columns for hours and find it exhilarating. The same is true of performers in television and film who talk of eighteen-hour days on the set and how this schedule feeds them.

Burnout rarely occurs when pursuing a strength. Top producers report that pressure and stress are in fact regenerative, often creating more energy. The practice of a strength is motivating and builds self-esteem.

WEAKNESSES: THE EIGHT CLUES

Another way to identify a weakness is by listening to the phrases you utter during the day. If you can recognize any or all of these in yourself, it's likely that you are practicing some weaknesses.

1. I've got to go to work versus I get to go to work.

2. When do I get off work? versus What am I to achieve today?

3. I want to work fewer hours versus There are not enough hours to do what I want to do.

4. I have a "job" versus I have a way of life.

5. I avoid work by drinking, overeating, gambling, using drugs, and calling in sick versus I think of ways to improve my performance at work even when I'm not actually there.

6. I have to force myself to work versus I feel energized from work.

7. I dislike my co-workers versus I have friends at work.

8. I have unrealistic expectations of what can be accomplished at work versus I have a set of objectives and a track record of achieving them.

THE OWNERSHIP PROCESS

It's one thing to write and talk about weaknesses, but it's another to claim them. How often do people buy and read diet books and never actually go on the food plan? How often do we read management books and never use any of the advice? Often. That won't do here. From our in-depth leadership interviews we know that successful leaders are quick to claim and manage weaknesses. Others, however, may get caught in a variety of psychological traps that keep the weaknesses alive and well. There are two psychological roadblocks individuals regularly experience.

Roadblock #1: Self-Perception

You've no doubt experienced a moment of truth with a friend who is devoted to some type of self-improvement, say singing lessons. After many months of intensive work, your friend shows no obvious improvement. After listening to her bemoan the cost and time involved with the lessons, you say, "Why don't you just give up on singing and try something else?" To the person whose self-image is *not attached* to the activity, your statement may bring an instant feeling of relief, a kind of permission to stop. This is a person who can still feel whole once she has let go of an impossible dream.

On the other hand, if your friend's self-concept is rooted in becoming the next Madonna or Beverly Sills, she's apt to be indignant at your advice. "I wouldn't think of stopping. I'll show you when I get my first recording contract." (We see this syndrome regularly with would-be actors who hold on to their dream of "one day becoming a star" years after their lack of talent is apparent to everyone else but themselves.) It's true that a confrontational statement such as "Why don't you just forget it and get a real job?" can often spur talented people on to greatness. It brings out the "I'm going to show 'em" response, causing them to double their efforts. In that case, the challenge is a powerful stimulus. But in many cases, it's the person without talent with great misguided persistence who presses on trying to prove he or she can achieve excellence in an area where the person has no strengths, only dreams. The acid test between these two extremes is some type of measurable progress.

Roadblock #2: Society's Definition
Letting Go of the Shoulds

Could this be the nineties: Men should be good at fixing things around the house like Bob Vila, and women should be dazzling cooks and homemakers like Martha Stewart? What, pray tell, do we do if some of us are no good at these chores? Do we continue to work at getting good at them, or do we have the courage to manage them? Too often we continue, apologizing along the way for our continued failures, losing self-esteem in the process.

Don tells the story of his experience in woodworking class in college. The last assignment was to make a goblet on a lathe. He thought, "Anyone should be able to do this. I'm determined to get it right." But by semester's end he was far behind in the project. But that didn't faze him. "All I needed was a little more time." He asked his instructor if he could work on the project over Christmas vacation, which bought him ten more days. He attempted goblet after goblet. With near-predictable timing, the stem would snap when near completion. Finally, near the end of the year, he completed a successful goblet and presented it to his instructor for evaluation. After examining the goblet, his instructor gave it a grade of D. A D—how was it possible with all his superior marks in science, math, and psychology that Don could earn a D in woodworking? It was a lesson that ultimately led to his realizing that woodworking (and just about anything else mechanical) was one of his weaknesses. Letting go of this traditional "male should" did not diminish his male identity. Rather it allowed him to focus his energies on his strengths.

In business, too, there are expectations: "Everyone should strive to become a manager" and eventually president or CEO of an organization, an idea well documented in the 1970s best seller *The Peter Principle*. "Cal," for example, bought into that "move up or out" management philosophy and worked as an insurance company manager for twelve years. While Cal was competent, we helped him discover his real strengths were in direct sales. He made the transition from management to sales, has quadrupled his income over the past five years, and enjoys unmatched satisfaction from his work. Management should be the ultimate goal for those with talents for it. The ultimate destination for those with strengths in other fields *is* other fields. The keep-at-it-at-any-cost idea is hammered into us from preschool on, and our very value system is often wrapped around the belief that "real men don't fail" and "good women never give up." We merely keep on trying until we master the situation. When the situation is positive and strengths are present, this dictum plays a powerful and indispensable role in moving us forward. But when we're working in an area of weakness, the philosophy locks us into a pattern where, like Doberman pinschers, we hold on no matter what.

Quickly admitting weak areas is an act of courage and growth. Those who embrace their nonstrengths are those who move on with developing their strengths.

THE FIVE STRATEGIES FOR MANAGING WEAKNESSES

Identifying a weakness is only the first half of the process. The second step involves the following five strategies: sloughing, subcontracting, complementary partnering, support systems, and alternatives.

Strategy No. 1: Sloughing

Sloughing is the easiest strategy to understand. It may, however, be the most difficult to put into practice. It means to find out what you don't do well and stop doing it—stop putting yourself in situations where you consistently fail. Stop running for elections you cannot win. Stop going to lunch with people whose attention you do not get. Stop going to meetings that aren't effective. Stop wasting time that could be applied in constructive pursuits.

Here is a two-part process to help you determine what activities could be sloughed:

1. Make a list of all the unenjoyable things you've done during the past six months.

2. Of those, which activities did not make a

difference to your life, even though they got done?

Evaluate the activities that end up on both lists for possible sloughing. Those could be: attending all meetings you were invited to attend; sending thank-you letters to people you met at conferences; attending all store openings; and reading copies of every sales call report.

Sloughing also extends to relationships. Have you ever been involved in a relationship—either business or personal—that had once brought out your imagination and courage and now only brings forth depression and anger? Society promotes as heroic the process of "holding on" even while opportunity slips away and misery takes its place. Magazines promote this heroism in articles under the banner "Can this marriage be saved?" This is a variation of the same "Can this partnership be saved? Can this working relationship be saved?" People tolerate the existence of negative relationships every day. But should they?

Lee Iacocca faced disappointment when Henry Ford II passed him over for the chairmanship of Ford. He and Ford had had a business relationship for years, and Iacocca had worked toward the chairmanship for well over a decade. Iacocca didn't hold on to failed dreams. He had the courage to end the partnership and take hold of the reins of the troubled Chrysler Corporation, where he built a powerful management team and made business history.

Now juxtapose Iacocca's action with that of the painter van Gogh, who sold only one painting during his lifetime. How could his career have been altered if he had had the courage to slough the nonproductive partnership he had with his manager, his brother?

Holding on to something that doesn't work is not an act of strength, it is an act of blocking. It is perpetuating a weakness that stands in the way of strengths.

Strategy No. 2: Subcontracting

Subcontracting is the process we like to call "enlightened delegation." In subcontracting, a task or weakness is assigned to a person or organization that possesses strengths in that area. This contrasts with traditional delegation, where work is given to another person or organization without thinking of whether the talent to do the job is there.

Denise Cavanaugh, a Washington, D.C.,–based business consultant, tells of her years spent struggling with proposal writing. "I'm great at presenting material to groups and identifying clients' needs, but I'm really terrible at putting those ideas down on paper. It takes me forever, and I'm never satisfied." After years of struggling with this glaring weakness and allowing it to consume large chunks of her time, she opted to hire a proposal writer, who whips out competent proposals in a fraction of the time she used to spend.

Dan Channing is a Dallas tax attorney who is a whiz in the courtroom. Yet he spent nearly a decade battling his finances. It seemed logical enough to him that a tax attorney should be capable of paying bills and handling taxes and investments. But each year, when April 15 began to close in, he would make a last-minute call to his accountant, asking for an extension in order to track down the necessary papers. Only after the IRS requested an audit did his wife force him to hire a bookkeeper, who now handles all the paperwork. Now Dan has perfect documentation for his year-end meeting with his accountant. At $10 an hour, the book-keeper is not a luxury but a money-making deal since Channing normally bills his professional time at $165 an hour. By subcontracting he is not only freed from the actual work but also from the worry and guilt that were by-products of the old system.

Strategy No. 3: Complementary Partnering

Complementary partnering is not what you think—the matching of one person's strengths to the other person's weaknesses and vice versa. It is rather the combining of each person's strengths to achieve a goal. This will create a magical outcome—a unique capability that could not be achieved by either person alone. It is the ultimate description of one plus one equals three. It is the teaming of strengths.

Some famous examples of complementary partnering are Fred Astaire and Ginger Rogers, Sears and Roebuck, George Burns and Gracie Allen, and Rodgers and Hammerstein.

Many new businesses are examples of complementary partnering where one person does the inside administration, the other one outside sales marketing and public relations.

Strategy No. 4: Support Systems

If you can find a way to make your life work better, use it. Everyone uses a support of some sort. For the person with poor eyesight, the support is eyeglasses; for the person with poor hearing, the support is a hearing aid. We view support systems as the way to function in our world. The trouble is that society often says fix it, you can overcome it, you don't need a crutch. So the airline pilot with poor depth perception performs eye exercises each day, believing he will achieve 20/20 sight. We say: *Use all the support systems you need to manage your weaknesses.*

- A Century City trial attorney who long suffered from hyperactivity and back problems had a stand-up desk built for his office and had all other equipment, including telephone and fax, set at standing height.

- Best-selling financial author William Donohugh is always challenged by new information for his television show and his books, and so he is constantly faced with paperwork—sorting clippings, notes, and scrap papers. To cut down the filing time he now travels with a laptop computer in which he stores story ideas and interview notes, often making inputs at airports.

- Noted for his horrible accident-prone driving, one CEO we interviewed hired a college student for $7 an hour to drive his Sedan DeVille, thereby eliminating stress and potential danger.

Support systems can also include the need for status symbols. One Wall Street executive we worked with felt embarrassed about his need for Savile Row suits and Mark Cross briefcases. He told us he should be able to function without these props. Should we even think of them as props? If status symbols bolster your confidence and make you feel good, why apologize for them? The same is true of titles. In the sixties, sensitivity training sessions often focused on people who identified themselves as Doctor. They were taunted unmercifully and told they should be secure enough to travel through life without any title. But why should society attempt to deny people a title they have earned, something that helps them complete their identity?

People with car phones often feel they have to justify their purchase by saying "The car phone is for road safety" rather than saying more honestly "My car phone is my ultimate toy . . . I enjoy it."

Strategy No. 5: Alternatives

Behavioral disorders such as dyslexia often block us from accomplishing our goals. In those cases, the support system is unique. The solution is to find an alternative way to accomplish the same task.

Roger Peters is an entrepreneur and founder of

Terratron, Inc., a company that owns and operates seventy-seven Hardee's franchises in the Midwest. Peters is typically brimming with ideas for the operation, but he doesn't verbalize those concepts. Instead, he appeals to his strengths and sketches them and in this way communicates his ideas to his people.

The point here is to identify your behavioral weakness and kick around other ideas for achieving the stated goal.

"Corinne," a manufacturing rep in Chicago, can talk up a storm with her customers but not with her partners. For years she infuriated her partners by using an attorney to negotiate her partnership agreements because she would become tongue-tied talking about percentages.

Following the death of her attorney, she finally decided to explore a different way of communicating her needs to her partners: preparing a proposal and working from that. Not only did she get a fair arrangement, but the proposal also improved her relationship with her partners. You can use different avenues to accomplish the same goals. It is every person's responsibility to be creative and to find those pathways.

YOU HIRE AS IS, YOU MARRY AS IS ... IF THE PERSON CHANGES, THAT'S A PLUS

Are we saying people never change? Are we saying weaknesses are constant? Typically, yes. There are, however, always exceptions, and dramatic transformations in behavior can take place.

For instance, the slovenly young man with a messy room who never combs his hair appears neat and well dressed one day. He does so not because he has worked at being neat and attractive, but because he has experienced a shift in his self-concept. He says to himself, "I'm not a child anymore. I'm a social human being who wants to have friends and be invited to parties." This young man has undergone the same process as the three-year-old thumb sucker who at the age of four no longer sucks his or her thumb. Why does someone's behavior change? Because there is a shift in the person's self-perception based on new demands that life makes.

An example could be made of a thirty-year-old young executive on the fast track who drinks too much and is known for his reckless behavior. One day he becomes "Mr. Responsibility" when he sees himself as a father and a parent. What appears to happen in one day is actually the result of several years. As the circumstances of his life change, so does the executive's self-image. He says, "I know that I'm living for the moment, indulging in drugs, food, drink, and sex, and I'd hate it if this behavior ever affected my kids." His old self-image is made up of all the rewards of living in the fast lane. The new picture has new rewards. It feels better to be home with the kids, going over homework every night rather than being out getting drunk with clients; it feels better to say no to drugs than to indulge. The man feels more rewarded by fatherhood than by fast living, and so he begins to see himself in a totally new way. His strengths have overwhelmed his weakness. But the weakness remains. What has changed is his lifestyle. Fatherhood has allowed his strengths to blossom, and there is little place in his life now where the weakness can gain a foothold.

Managing our weaknesses allows our strengths to overpower them, ultimately making them irrelevant.

THE BENEFITS OF CLAIMING YOUR WEAKNESSES

Once a weakness is identified and a management strategy is put in place for it, you are virtually free of it. Claiming weaknesses is the critical step to building strengths since weaknesses sap us of our time and energies. They rob us of the enthusiasm we derive from practicing our strengths, from doing what we do best.

Managing our weaknesses allows our strengths to overpower them, ultimately making them irrelevant.

PART TWO

PART TWO

The Strengths' Catalysts

Mark Twain told a wonderful story about one man's search for the world's greatest general. The man spent an entire lifetime looking for the general and finally the day came for him to travel on. When he arrived in heaven he walked over to St. Peter and said, "I'm looking for the world's greatest general."

St. Peter said, "I know, I know, we've been expecting you, and I have good news. If you'll look right over there, you will see the world's greatest general."

The old man excitedly looked over and said, "That is not the world's greatest general. That man was a cobbler on main street in my hometown!"

St. Peter responded, "But had he been a general, he would have been the greatest general ever."

Did the cobbler know this? Did he know his true strengths? Did he know he could have been the world's greatest general? Perhaps, like many people, the cobbler was not aware of his strengths. We need other people to know and recognize our strengths so we can become the best that is in us.

From our research we know that strengths atrophy and die when left alone. The best salespeople, managers, and company leaders are similar to the great athletes of the world in that their strengths do not develop in a vacuum. They require a set of what we term "catalysts" to bring them to life. We think of them as "chemical agents" that transform inert potential into active strengths. These catalysts are (1) mission, (2) relationship, (3) expectations, and (4) celebration. Lacking these catalysts, the cobbler is left working on the next pair of boots instead of in command of the troops. Part Two is dedicated to helping you understand how to use these catalysts to develop a strength. We will also discuss how to apply those same catalysts to developing the strengths of your partners, co-workers, children, and friends.

CHAPTER 5

Strengths Develop Best
in the Framework of Mission

As she explained in her book, *Mary Kay on People Management,* Mary Kay Ash didn't launch her cosmetics empire just for fun and profit; she had another force driving her, a mission:

> I had a product and I had the drive and energy to make my business successful, but I wanted one more thing . . . I wanted to help women achieve. My frustrations as a woman in the business world were based on the fact that I had often been paid far less than a man doing the same work. Many times I had trained a salesman and after months of guiding and teaching him on the road, he was brought back to Dallas and made my superior at twice my salary! The reason I was given was

that these men had families to support. No one seemed to care that I had a family to support also.

I wanted a company that would respect the contribution women could make. I knew we were smart and capable, honest and committed. Couldn't my new company recognize these talents? My company would offer women opportunities that in 1963 didn't exist anywhere else. I knew there was a vast, unlimited amount of talent and dedication to hard work that had never been tapped before—simply because these talented and dedicated people were women.

THE NATURE OF MISSION

Thomas Jefferson once said, "Never fear the want of business. Anyone who qualifies for a calling never fails of employment." Let us substitute the word mission for calling and explore for a moment this powerful and ethereal quality and how it provides the theater for strengths to perform.

Personal mission is rare, so rare that when we experience it, we refer to the person as having "It." The French even have a phrase for it, *je ne sais quoi,* or "that certain something." Personal mission is rare because we as a society do not promote it. We promote the development of goals to further our careers, we acknowledge the value of passion as a motivator, and we celebrate vision in our leaders, but mission gets chopped up into several traditional avenues:

1. In business, senior management sometimes crafts a corporate mission statement, a statement of purpose for the company (a task too few companies embrace).

2. Religion is another avenue that promotes mission.

3. The military talks of mission, conjuring up bombing raids and the taking of military positions.

4. Humanitarians such as Albert Schweitzer, Buckminster Fuller, or Mother Teresa embody mission.

These examples suggest that mission happens only on the big stage, but that assumption is false. Many of the top performers in our studies had their own mission. They felt that humankind could benefit from their work in various ways, and so they were driven. They also knew that missions were personal and not in any way limited solely to traditional humanitarian aims. Humanistic missions have been encouraged throughout the centuries. But what of the mission of building quality into a Xerox machine or a Cadillac Seville? Or of helping people feel secure by having the right Northwestern Mutual life insurance, or the perfect stay at the Ritz Carlton or Marriott? Cannot the desire to provide quality to people in a product or service also be a meaningful mission? We say yes. Mission must first be personal. Your mission must mean the world to you. When put together with your strengths, it becomes your fuel for achievement.

Andy Lipkis, the founder of Tree People, is one of our favorite success profiles. In the late seventies his mission was to save the hillsides of California. Volunteers from the Southern California area would replant trees after the annual fires. His mission helped him battle the state and federal bureaucracies, overcome red tape and funding rejections, and, through a stroke of inspiration, make the reforestation project happen. The turning point occurred when he took his plight to the media. On the *Merv Griffin Show* he presented his concept and spoke of the obvious benefits to the taxpayers of California. Several days after the show aired, he was granted funding. Today the Tree People save California taxpayers more than half a million dollars annually by using volunteers in the otherwise costly task of reforestation.

Dr. Bob Barkley, a nationally known leader in the field of dentistry, dramatically illustrates the importance of mission. His observations of his profession led him to describe the prevailing dental practice as "Drill, fill, and bill."

Early in his career, a young woman came to Dr. Barkley's office. She asked to have all her teeth pulled and replaced by dentures. It was a shocking request from a woman who was in her thirties and very attractive. Nevertheless, she explained she had been urged by her family to deal with her "soft teeth" now "before you run up big dental bills." Soft teeth were an inherited trait that had affected many of her closest family members and nearly always ended in the removal of teeth and their replacement with dentures.

"Do it now, and save yourself thousands of dollars in dental bills," her husband and family told her.

Dr. Barkley didn't agree. He had promised himself he would never extract a tooth, because almost all teeth could be restored. He came up with an alternative strategy that included a nutritional and maintenance plan and a few technical steps that would allow her to keep her teeth for her entire lifetime. It would cost $1,200. He thought he had convinced her to take the preventive route. She said she wanted to think it over. Six months later he saw her at the local shopping mall. Her teeth had all been pulled, and she was toothless. The sight of her led to a watershed in his life. He could think only of her loss of self-esteem. He suddenly knew his purpose in life was not "Drill, fill, and bill." His mission became *to help people claim their self-esteem*.

He went on to accomplish his mission by helping dentists feel their mission for getting patients to take responsibility for themselves through caring for their oral health. This, he reasoned, would enhance their self-esteem throughout their lives.

His mission was not a solitary pursuit, but a message he shared with fellow dentists around the world through lectures, books, and seminars until his untimely death in an airplane accident in 1975. Many dentists who had been bored with their profession (the drilling, filling, and billing ones) were ignited by Dr. Barkley's mission and took up their work with new vigor, challenged to teach each patient to "own" his own health. Dr. Barkley's mission, like his memory, is his legacy that lives on in the minds and hearts of all who met him or have heard his thoughts. Such is the power of mission.

Mission and the Bottom Line

Though mission seems like a spiritual pursuit, it can have an impact on worldly matters.

Even in our studies of insurance sales agents, we found that some of the top performers felt guided by a sense of mission. They would see an insured family where the father had died and feel satisfaction because they contributed to the family's ability to stay together and educate the children.

Some great insurance agents are so driven by mission that they were moved to tears during interviews because they were so concerned for someone they could not help.

When Mission Grows Thin, Organizations Deteriorate

Peter Drucker has said that foremost in the minds of executives must be the reality that their organization exists because it serves people outside of their organization.

When companies think only of how many units they can produce or sell, something happens to the spirit of the organization, and sales decrease rather than increase.

When the Detroit automakers focused only on how many cars they could move rather than how well they could serve the American people with quality transportation (their mission), they lost 30 percent of the market share.

When hospitals think only of how to fill their beds rather than how to be a quality place for people to claim their health, they have financial problems.

This phenomenon has been so clear in our study of companies that we voice strong concern whenever an organization, whether business, church, or school, emphasizes selling units over providing quality service to customers.

In business, when a manager communicates a genuine sense of mission to co-workers, profits and productivity usually follow. The more frequently a salesperson speaks of his or her mission, the higher his or her sales will be. Mission and profits are interdependent.

Mission as Motivator

Selling can be a selfish experience, serving the seller more than the customer. Mission is the antidote to selfishness.

When strengths are driven by mission, a circle is

created. Strengths feed mission. For example, a sales-person's desire to contribute to the world by selling medical supplies is a mission. But it is put into practice by his or her sales strengths. The successful use of these strengths creates a pleasant feeling of satisfaction in the salesperson, which reinforces the sense of mission. And so we emphasize that "strengths function best in the framework of mission."

Goals Die; Mission Lives On

Mission is at the heart of why you do what you do. Goals, on the other hand, are often the steps to its achievement. Mission is altruistic. A goal does not necessarily have to better the world. Mission has an eternal quality—the benefits often extend far beyond a lifetime. Goals are timebound. They die because they are achieved, to be replaced by others. Memorable po-litical leaders often had a mission. Getting elected was only one goal in the achievement of it.

Roark Stratton told us recently of a conversation he had with an SRI client who explained that his mis-sion was "to be number one." That's not a corporate mission statement; that's a corporate goal. A true mis-sion statement expresses the company's *raison d'être,*

> **A true mission statement expresses the company's *raison d'être*, the purpose for its existence, and often becomes the invisible life force that drives and unifies.**

the purpose for its existence, and often becomes the invisible life force that drives and unifies.

The mission statement at Federal Express is brief, elegant, and obviously effective: "Help the world through better and faster communications." At the Menninger Foundation in Topeka, Kansas, the mission statement is elaborate and eloquent:

Improving the quality of life . . .
By developing, utilizing and disseminating
psychiatric knowledge.
To help people who are ill
as well as those who are not ill
find greater personal fulfillment and satisfaction
through personal autonomy and enhanced capacity
to cope with the stress of life.

The Ringling Bros.' Mission of Amusement, first penned in 1899, is heartfelt and long lasting:

> To be good, mankind must be happy. To wreathe the face of humanity in smiles for a time, to loosen the chains that hold man captive to his duties and return him to them better fitted for his obligations, is the mission of amusement and the one great desire of moralists is, and ought to be, that it be pure and wholesome.
>
> Amusement unfetters the mind from its environs and changes the dreary monotony of the factory's spindles to the joyous song of the meadowlark. It gives flight to the caged soul to treat in airy places. It softens the wrinkles of sorrow, makes smiles of frowns.
>
> This is the mission of amusement—and the circus, with its innocent sights of joy for the children and its power to make all men and women children again for at least one day, comes the nearest of any form of amusement to fulfilling this mission.

A MISSION, NOT A GOAL: DESIGNING YOUR OWN MISSION STATEMENT

As we begin this exercise, which may involve a few minutes or many months, let us state clearly the purpose: to write a personal or corporate mission statement that will help you to focus your strengths.

We would like to ask you to set aside some time (not necessarily now) to answer the following question in writing: *What is it that you believe you do that makes a difference to other people and to mankind? or, in other words, Why do you do what you do?*

Write fast—don't worry about spelling, logic, or grammar. The objective is to let your thoughts flow. Remember, we are not talking about goals here, we are talking about mission. Your quest is to define your life purpose.

When you have finished, go back and look over your words. You can then begin to edit them.

Let's clarify some immediate questions that nearly always arise:

1. *How long should a mission statement be?*

A mission statement should be simple enough to be remembered and frequently reflected upon. The length of the mission statement can be anywhere from one paragraph to several pages—provided you can summarize its essence. One restaurateur, in referring to his mission statement, simply said, "To delight our customers."

2. *Should your mission statement show how the mission is to be accomplished?*

No. A mission statement does not show actual plans. It is designed to direct and express your values and beliefs. It provides guides, not goals.

3. *Should everyone (in a company) have a mission statement?*

Ideally, yes, though naturally the statements will not all be the same, but there should be commonality.

4. *Does everyone have to believe or agree with your mission?*

No. The goal is not to proselytize or convert, but to express your true desires without regard to what others will think. Often others with a mission will be supportive of yours since they understand the value of having one. People without a mission may also be supportive if yours fits with their beliefs. (Hence the power of a leader with a popular mission!) People want to follow a person who knows where he or she is going.

However, there will always be detractors. Some people may not understand the importance of mission and how it relates to success. Those lacking purpose in their own lives may feel compelled to dismiss your purpose or even feel negative about it.

5. *Do mission statements change over the years?*

Ideally, yes. If you begin your life or career with an awareness of mission, you can assume that it will grow as you grow. You may even find you take on several missions that relate to different areas of your life.

6. *Do one's mission and work have to coincide?*

If our work gives us purpose, then we have an advantage. But many people have a mission separate from their work, and their job is the means to support it. Here are some examples:

- Kent Pelz, a banker in Los Angeles, devotes twenty hours a week to world peace.

- Ann Blank, a single mother in Chicago, works as an executive secretary to fund her mission—the education of her children.

- Jane Fonda uses her earnings from acting to fund humanitarian and political campaigns.

- Paul Newman launched Newman's Own food products line to generate profits for his favorite causes.

Here are some typical mission statements:

- Life Insurance Agent: To provide financial security to families.

- Clothing Salesperson: To help people look their best.

- Farmer: To provide food for people of the world.

- Manager: To help people develop their capabilities.

- Law Enforcement Officer: To help people understand lawfulness and live together lawfully, and to give them security in their neighborhood communities.

LIVING A MISSION STATEMENT

Claim Your Mission

As we said earlier, personal mission is rare. To live a mission requires that you realize you can make a difference in this world. It also requires that you practice the strengths to fulfill your mission. Writing and developing your mission statement is neither instant nor easy. It's not like choosing a style of bank checks for your new account. Discovering that inner drive and matching it with real-world activities requires time and the commitment to your drives and needs. Mission statements can grow out of a strong sense of responsibility or a strong sense of rage. Leaders of the women's movement are clearly driven by mission, motivated by legal and financial inequities. Environmentalists are motivated by a sense of responsibility to future inhabitants of the earth. Some corporate leaders, on the other hand, have a mission about literacy motivated by their belief that a competitive workforce is a literate one.

Talk Your Mission Whenever You Get a Chance

"I just sold that lady her first Cadillac, and I know she's going to be happy."

"It was really exciting to see the looks on their faces when they understood that success and failure, strengths and weaknesses, were not opposites."

These statements are examples of talking mission. The Cadillac salesman has a mission to help people have safe, reliable transportation. To him the discussion of a Cadillac sale is talking his mission statement.

Enjoy Your Mission

Mission, like exercise, is most effective when experienced as often as possible. A person exercising his or her strengths on a daily basis is both developing strengths and fulfilling a sense of purpose. It becomes a win/win situation. Mission statements that live only on paper are a win/lose proposition. Having a mission statement and not living it is perhaps worse than having no mission at all. The only result would be guilt.

MISSION: THE ULTIMATE EMPOWERER

You are talking with your seatmate on a cross-country flight. During the conversation it becomes clear that your seatmate is very successful. In the course of your mile-high chat, you learn about his lifestyle, including not-so-passing references to his house, car, swimming pool, private schools, and all the requisite perks of success. But as the conversation progresses the tone switches from one of apparent satisfaction to one of emptiness, conjuring up the haunting message of the old Peggy Lee song, "Is That All There Is?" Your seatmate is the victim of a common syndrome: the search for purpose. Life goals have been reached, the brass ring has been won, and suddenly the question is "Now what?"

As the great leaders know, mission is the resolution to this malaise.

Mission gives purpose to life. It adds meaning to what one does. In its purest form, it is so deeply felt that it explains why one does what one does. One's mission will touch the heart versus the head. A mission must benefit the world.

Mission is a quality made most vivid by the great leaders of the world, from Jesus Christ to contemporary leaders. Consider President John F. Kennedy's famous statement, "Ask not what your country can do for you, ask what you can do for your country."

Dr. Martin Luther King, Jr., spoke from a sense of mission with his refrain "I have a dream, I have a dream."

President Bush conveyed it in his inaugural address when he made reference to his famous "thousand points of light."

Each of these statements captured the imagination and hearts of millions and is appropriately etched in the pages of history. The power of mission is well known to leaders who realize that humankind has a longing for it. Lacking a mission, people are likely to have only materialistic goals. But mission is not the exclusive territory of great leaders. It is the right of every person interested in developing his or her strengths, and it's one of the essential ingredients of excellence.

CHAPTER 6

Strengths Develop Only in Relation to Another Human Being

Lib Hatcher, a former Charlotte, North Carolina, restaurant owner, had an experience on the night of August 1, 1981, that changed her life forever. "I was standing at the sideboard working on some papers. As soon as I heard the first notes out of his mouth I dropped my pen and papers, the sound was that astounding."

At the time, Randy Travis was a seventeen-year-old singer with a history of drinking too much and getting into trouble. Lib hired him on the spot and spent the next nine years of her life believing in his ability to break through to the big time. Working with him daily, she bankrolled a demo record, made contacts in the record industry, and even moved to Nashville, ending her marriage along the way, to give Travis better access to record company executives. In 1985 an executive from CBS records in New York was in the audience at Lib's new Nashville night spot. The following day he signed Travis to a recording contract. Today Travis, managed by Lib Hatcher, has won three Country Music of the Year awards and has sold more than 43 million albums. Lib Hatcher's belief in Travis's strength developed a singer whom, without her investment, the world could have missed.

RELATIONSHIP

Although we recognize that negative relationships exist (a point we discuss later in this chapter), we define "relationship" in its most positive light:

Relationship is the process of investing in another person by doing things for that person's own good without consideration of self-reward. Ultimately, it is the sum of our responses to another human being.

The fabric of our lives is constructed person by person. As our relationships increase, we benefit geometrically: Our lives become richer, and we expand our strengths through others.

THE MIXED MESSAGES OF RELATIONSHIP

How is it then that relationships in the workplace are considered unimportant? While coaches and trainers are often credited with the success of Olympic athletes, similar relationships in business and education are rarely valued as a tool for sharpening the bottom line. How can this dichotomy be explained? Easily, when you consider our popular cultural myths:

1. Don't get too close to your people, you may have to fire them.

2. Don't let your boss know too much about you, he or she may use it against you.

3. Familiarity breeds contempt.

4. If you want it done right, do it yourself.

5. You have to make it on your own.

These rules may be okay for those weak in relationship skills or those with poor judgment, but the truly outstanding performers are those who are secure in their relationships and won't be limited by these rules.

IF MAN IS AN ISLAND, WHO NEEDS A RELATIONSHIP?

The image of the rugged individualist, from the Marlboro Man to John Wayne and Amelia Earhart, seems to downplay the need for anything but self-sufficiency. But relationships play a critical role in human development beginning with the first days of life. Margaret A. Ribble, in her work entitled "Clinical Studies of Instinctive Relation in Newborn Babies," found that children who weren't held enough early in life developed apathy, physical deformation, and ultimately never grew to their full potential. But the importance of relationships doesn't end in the crib, it matters for a lifetime.

From our Organizational Development Analysis (ODA), a questionnaire in which employees are asked about their attitudes toward their corporate environments, we have learned the following:

1. A 1990 study of radio stations sponsored by New City Communications of Worcester, Massachusetts, showed that the stations with the greatest profits have the highest percentage of employees with best friends at work.

2. A 1981 study for Golden Corral Restaurants showed that when employees thought their

manager cared about them, customers gave the restaurant a better customer service rating.

3. In exit interviews for agents of Mutual of Omaha, the most common reason given for agents voluntarily terminating employment was "My manager didn't care about me."

Strengths develop best in response to another human being.

So relationships are hardly inconsequential to the bottom line. They are like yeast to dough, a critical agent in the development of people's strengths. The goal of this chapter is to show how strengths develop best in response to another human being. The stronger your relationships, the more rapidly your strengths and the strengths of your employees will develop.

YOUR PERSONAL
BOARD OF DIRECTORS

We would like to invite you to perform an exercise we regularly use in our seminars. Draw a large oval on a sheet of paper. Imagine this represents the table in your life board of directors' room. Put yourself at the head of the table as chairperson. Now write the names of your personal board of directors around the table. These people will quickly come to mind. They are the significant persons in your life. They may never have been together in the same room. They have you in common. These board members are the persons you meet with when you have to make important decisions. You can feel their approval of your successes and feel their empathy when you have problems. How many you place around the table is up to you.

Participants generally list three to fifteen people. People of all ages sit around the table—some of short acquaintance, some of long acquaintance. Some are no longer alive but still have an influence on you. Typical members of this board of directors include:

1. Family members—parents, spouse, children

2. Best friend(s)

3. Current or former manager

4. Teacher(s)

5. Pastor/Priest/Rabbi

6. Lawyer/Accountant

When the exercise has been completed, we ask four questions:

1. *Do the people on your board of directors know they are members?*

Typically, the answer is no. But why not let those board members know? Let them know what the exercise means. Sharing this news will make an indelible impression on them and will probably strengthen your relationships. You could thank them for ways they have helped you. Wouldn't it be wonderful if someone thanked you for including him or her and told you what an honor it was? Try it.

2. *If the people with whom you work did this exercise, would you want them to put you on their board?*

If the answer is yes, you might think about behaving in ways that would cause them to keep you on their board or to invite you to be on their board. Wanting to earn a position on their boards can help us behave in winning ways.

3. *Who isn't on your board who should be?*

Are there people who could make a dramatic difference in your future if you added them to your board? If so, this is the time to identify those people and take whatever steps necessary to "bring them on board." Early in Don's career he consciously developed a relationship with the late Dr. J. McVicker Hunt, the esteemed psychologist, who supported Don's research and theory. This was a relationship that didn't just happen by circumstances but one that Don pointedly sought and developed. It is also one that Don treasures to this day.

4. *What best explains these successful relationships?*

In almost all cases, we have positive relationships with those on our board of directors. These are some of our best, our most successful relationships. Our goal should be to have more like them. So we should carefully examine the characteristics of these relationships. Beside each name on your board of directors, write the first reason you can think of that explains why that person has a special place on your board. Typical reasons are: they trust me, I trust them, they care about me, we are honest with each other, I learn from them, they are mentors. After you have put a reason or two by each person, ask yourself what is common among all of the reasons. If you find something in common, and most people do, you have discovered a strength in building relationships that you should rely on to build many more relationships.

Relationship helps us to define who we are and what we can become. Most of us can trace our successes to pivotal relationships.

Early in Paula's career, Peter Stanton, a successful entrepreneur and financial wizard from Harvard, introduced her to the world of business and helped her to know that she could be successful. Several years later, after she co-founded three companies and took one public, another friend and business associate, George Otis, helped her to believe that she should become an author. He subsequently became the godfather of her first book, *The Joy of Money*. Relationship helps us to define who we are and what we can become. Most of us can trace our successes to pivotal relationships.

A BOARD OF DIRECTORS
FOR YOUR CAREER

Just as you created a life board, you can use the same technique to create a career board. You identify two or three people who will help you build on your strengths and ask them to serve on your career board. Most people will feel honored to be asked. You talk to them every six months for an hour or so about your activities of the past six months, how you have achieved your goals, and what you plan to do in the next six months. We have found that when you let other people know what you are trying to do, they will usually try to help you. Don't dismiss this concept as merely goal-planning sessions; it is an opportunity to solidify your relationships and reflect upon your strengths.

MANAGING RELATIONSHIPS;
BUILDING STRENGTHS

Every person has to manage his or her own relationships. (The day you discover this fact is a great day, a turning point in your life.)

You can leave your money in a checking account or invest it wisely. Building relationships is an investment process. Your goal is to maximize your return on relationship investment (RORI). A *laissez-faire* attitude toward the development and maintenance of relationships will net you a low RORI. The highest returns will be earned by those who assertively manage their relationships.

THE NINE PRINCIPLES FOR MANAGING RELATIONSHIPS

Principle #1: Think of Others in Terms of Their Strengths

Ask first: "What strengths do you have that I can relate to?" Keeping in mind the strengths of the other person will empower that person and greatly enhance your relationship.

If you say to a person, "Last night I was thinking about you. I figured out five things you do wrong when you make a speech. When may I go over these mistakes with you?" will that person want to get together with you?

Compare that with saying, "Last night I was admiring the way you make speeches. I discovered four strengths you have in speaking. Would you like to hear what they are?"

Which scenario is more appealing to you? For most people it is the latter.

When you focus on people's strengths, they will want to talk to you and spend time learning about you, perhaps discovering your strengths. You will help your friends take pride in their strengths. Such an attitude places the relationships on a positive footing and sets the tone for success in an organization. Leaders around the world are thinking about empowerment these days, and there is no more effective way to empower people than to see each person in terms of his or her strengths.

Principle #2: Quality Relationships Develop One on One

Relationships develop in two primary ways: in groups and individually. In a group you attain a sense of belonging, but in a one-to-one relationship intimacy and trust can flourish. Our best relationships have developed only on a one-to-one basis. That means giving 100 percent attention to the other person.

This process is the same, for example, with salespeople. Managers should spend time with each top salesperson individually, learning how that person thinks and feels about work. And with a spouse or co-worker, the most valuable times together take place on a one-to-one basis and should be of the other person's design.

In a family, most of the time is of the adults' design. Parents take children along on the parents' errands. Yet with children the most memorable times are those where the parent *spent time individually with a child, doing what the child wanted to do.* The activity may be watching television together in his or her room, going shopping at his or her favorite store, or sorting through baseball cards or CDs in the basement. That is why it's so important to offer others "their" time. An hour per week with each child, each salesperson, or each co-worker is the minimum investment necessary to build a solid relationship. Making that happen on a regular basis requires the same type of scheduling techniques used for business meetings. Try it.

Does it always have to be on their turf? Yes, for at least an hour a week, if the goal is building relationships.

Principle #3: "Doing For" Never Makes Up for "Doing With"

We cheat relationships when we only do things *for* another person rather than *with* them. For instance, how often do we substitute giving things for time? When parents return from a business trip, they assuage their guilt by bringing gifts for the children or spouse. We send "gifts" to friends rather than schedule time to sit and talk. CEOs overpay their associates, binding them with golden handcuffs, rather than developing them.

The same thing happens in other ways. Successful parents use their contacts to get a job for their child or a place in college rather than helping them earn their place. To the child, it can feel like an unearned reward.

But there's more. We *do for* others in the area of emotional issues. When someone we care about has a problem, our knee-jerk reaction is to fix it. Not only does the fix-it process rarely work, but it also inhibits bonding and creates a relationship based on manipulation. If an associate is sad, we try to change him and make him happy because we don't know how to deal with his sadness. If a friend is having a problem, we try to help her problem disappear so we can feel more comfortable.

Doing with people means accepting them in whatever emotional state they may be in, being constantly aware of their strengths, and respecting that they are responsible for the resolution *and* for their own growth. *The empowering act is to hurt with them when they're sad or troubled and be elated with them in their successes. By sharing feelings with people, you bond with them and give them a sense of warmth and consolation.*

Principle #4: The More People Know About Each Other, the More Likely They Are to Like Each Other

The famous English author Charles Lamb told of a quick interchange that took place between him and a friend while walking down a street in his hometown:

"I don't like that man."

"You don't even know that man," Lamb replied.

"That's why I don't like that man."

In a week-long study performed on tax attorneys at the Nebraska Center for Continuing Education, we found that on the morning of the big exam, the lawyers who took the time to get to know each other at the beginning of the conference had a higher score on the content exam and had significantly more positive attitudes. Participants considered their higher scores to be the result of getting together and talking about the content. The more you learn about another person, the more likely it is that you will find some common ground.

Here are some suggestions for learning more about a person:

1. Learn a person's name, specifically the name he or she wants to be called.

2. Find out what the person gets paid to do.

3. Learn what excites the person—family, pets, politics, golf, and so on.

4. Discover one of the person's strengths.

5. Discern what the person *wants* to do. What are his goals? How does she see the future?

Principle #5: There Is No Trust Without Risk

Most relationships are low risk. Our relationships with the people we see each day, even the people with whom we work closely, rarely have a high level of risk. We don't share confidences, go out of our way to help each other, or lend significant amounts of money to each other.

Risk falls into two categories: situational risk and shared risk. War provides an ideal theater for *situa-*

tional risk when buddies are thrown together in a life-and-death setting emotionally charged by a powerful mission. Situational risk occurs during times of disaster and emergency when people pull together and often develop friendships that can last a lifetime.

Shared risk relies solely on the integrity of those involved. A shared risk can be a confidence about the status of your marriage or the details of a pending lawsuit or a possible promotion. Sharing a confidence brings with it an expectation—that the confidence will be valued and remain between the two of you. Sharing risk also includes acts such as buying a house with a partner, launching a company together, or signing a contract with another person. Shared risk strengthens a relationship. For without risk, there can be no trust.

Principle #6: Relationships Are Built One Commitment at a Time

Psychologist Frank Brown describes a mature relationship in terms of commitment: "A mature relationship is one where both parties do what they say they will do." How startlingly basic and how patently true. The issue is not about disorganization; people can relate to organized confusion if it's the norm. What friends and co-workers cannot tolerate is inconsistent behavior and broken promises. How many times have you waited for a promised telephone call only to receive no word? There follows a lessening in the value of the relationship. But by holding to your promises, you show respect for the other person's time and involvement. Take something as minor as a dinner date set for 6:30 P.M. on a Thursday. If the date is missed, it can feel like an assault on the relationship. If this happens regularly, failed promises and broken appointments nearly always lead to failed relationships.

Principle #7: Being Liked Is Important

Of all the people interviewed as prospective managers by SRI in 1990, only 40 percent answered positively to the question "Do you work at getting others to like you?" Many respondents claimed that they weren't running a popularity contest and had only one goal: to be respected. Interestingly, that attitude serves no one but the respondent. Respect is for one's self. Liking is for others. When others can like you, it is easier and more productive for them to work with you. Wanting to be liked is the first step to being liked. (True, people like Scrooge can attempt to exist without people, but even he had a vision and changed his ways.)

In *Kids Don't Learn from People They Don't Like,*

author and educator David Aspy finds that when students don't like a teacher, they develop a resistance to learning from him or her. In our research, we discovered that the best teachers are liked by their students. Is it any different in corporate environments where employees or co-workers don't like their supervisors or managers? Our study of employee surveys shows that when managers or leaders are liked, there is better attendance, retention, service quality, and productivity. Here are four specific steps to promote likability:

1. *Help people get to know you.* Share anecdotes about your life, including both positive and painful stories. The goal is to be open so that others may learn about you and be sensitive to you.

2. *Recognize the success of others.* A sale, the completion of a project, or work well done is a reason to send a note, give a pat on the back, or plan a small celebration to highlight another's achievements. Well-timed congratulations last for a long, long while.

3. *Let others know you like them.* In the 1990 study of SRI seminar training sessions, it was found that seminar leaders who told participants that they liked them had higher scores on their overall evaluations. Studies show that doctors, teachers, nurses, and managers who pointedly let co-workers, students, and patients "know they like them" enjoy better results

than those who say nothing. How often do we take time to let the people we work with know how much we like them?

4. *Be a good listener.* Listen until the other person feels good. Because listening is so scarce, a little of it goes a long way. Good listening gives full attention to the other person. Nodding, frequent "mmhmms," and asking good questions lets the other person know you are aware.

Principle #8: Relationships Don't Just Happen; Be an Activator

Relationship building is not a spectator sport; it is not a passive activity. It requires initiative as opposed to what has been termed "cocooning." A cocooner's day runs something like this: He gets into his car in the garage, drives alone to work, walks down the hall to his office, closes the door, his secretary screens calls, and then he drives home, only to stay inside, cut off from the world. Being an activator means taking the lead—you don't wait for people or events to happen to you.

In Gail Sheehy's book *Character,* she cites the activator role of President George Bush, who reportedly spends two hours each night writing notes to friends, family, partners, and acquaintances. Closeness requires actions such as casual hellos, setting times to get together, having "good talks," dropping congratulatory notes, and making informal phone calls.

One way to extend your relationships is to learn the names of many people who work in your company, go to your church, or are members of your club, and then call them by name every time you see them.

Principle #9: Use Relationship Strengths, Manage Your Weaknesses

Relationship strengths are a unique part of you. President John F. Kennedy possessed several relationship strengths. One was eloquence. His personal charisma was another. He used it to win friends and influence voters.

Malcolm Forbes's relationship strengths were his love of parties and his desire to dazzle his guests. Another famous party giver of the sixties, Perle Mesta, was able to select and mix interesting people, which made her parties social events of the year. She was often quoted as saying "If you want a really good party, you invite the right people."

But there are other forms of relationship strengths that may happen in less dramatic ways. Here are several

CLIFTON AND NELSON

profiles that we hope will help you know and use your relationship strengths.

We mentioned Dr. Clifford Hardin, former Secretary of Agriculture and chancellor of the University of Nebraska. Not only does he have a powerful résumé, but he is also a powerful *nurturer*. At last count, his proudest achievement is the fact that sixteen of his university administrative interns, with whom he worked closely, have become university and college presidents. Over the years, he has kept a watchful eye out for those with leadership qualities and has made a pointed effort to cultivate them.

Nurturing is a strength that resembles the best kind of parenting. A manager or teacher gains satisfaction from the growth of employees or students. The nurturer is excited when an employee makes a sale or an associate learns a new skill, earns a promotion, buys a new home, or announces the birth of a baby. The nurturer can "see" each increment of growth and expresses heartfelt warmth that enables employees to grow.

Ida Stewart, a vice president with Estee Lauder, is a *wooer*. At conventions or parties, she effortlessly "works the room," gracefully moving from person to person, exchanging greetings and business cards.

In her sales work, this strength is an instant benefit: It allows her to quickly establish rapport in virtually any situation. She would not flourish in a job in which she had no contact with new people.

Wooers continuously work to get people to approve of them. This is not a sign of weakness or neurosis but an invaluable quality in people who work with customers. Such managers get to know their co-workers one by one and develop a positive rapport with them. They evaluate themselves according to how well they think their co-workers regard them. Nonwooers will often rationalize that their goal is to get co-workers to "respect them." Wooers are the most valuable people you can have when it comes to winning customers in the retail business, for instance, or in sales. Their goal: to make friends as quickly as possible.

Similarly, *courtiers* are artists in human relations who know how to gain the favor of others to achieve a specific goal. They use charm, timing, compliments, and gifts to get things done. They have an intuitive sense for the proper dress and the right remark. They take time to figure people out and then make moves as strategic and purposeful as a master chess player's to balance relationships in their favor. Courtliness is a strength of great achievers and leaders who can get people to champion their ideas. They know the difference between thinking and emotion and can at times be cold and calculating about their goals. It is the mark of the politician, entrepreneur, leader, and crack salesperson. It is also the mark of a con man and manipulator à la J. R. Ewing when used in the negative sense.

Nurses who give painless injections are *empathizers,* or have the ability to sense the feelings of another person. In the case of injections, the nurse shares the pain by hurting with the patient, thereby easing or eliminating the pain. When a person listens to you and expresses an understanding of your feelings, rapport is enhanced. Empathy builds trust quickly. Think of the power of this strength in sales, the helping professions, and leadership. One sales manager we studied had such extraordinary empathy he could "feel" with his salespeople as they were out in the field and sense what each of their calls was like. It was as if he were right there with them. He could finish the sentences of his salespeople as they told about their calls. Those with empathy are active listeners who make their listeners feel heard.

Those with the strength of *individualized perception* can see the drama in other people's lives and often communicate in stories. Life to them is a drama. Authors such as Belva Plain know well the value of individualized perception for writers—it allows them to develop a character, to hear the melodies in people's lives, and write about them so there is a consistency in the character.

Managers who are stimulators help employees feel good about themselves and their work. Managers stimulate co-workers in a variety of ways, such as recognizing good work, telling dramatic or humorous stories, or talking in meetings about company mission. Stimulators have the ability to stir emotions, and they have a sense of humor, an element of "show biz."

RELATIONSHIP REALITIES: NOT ALL RELATIONSHIPS ARE POSITIVE

From the barrage of statistics chronicling the turnover rate of employees in Corporate America and the number of failed marriages, we know that not all relationships work. That is a fact we recognize each time we enter into a relationship, whether personal or professional.

One of the most famous working relationships to sour in recent years is the Scully/Jobs Apple partnership. Scully's book *Odyssey* chronicled in detail the elaborate "courting process" Jobs undertook to woo Scully to join Apple. It was to be a partnership made in corporate heaven. But while it seemed positive at the beginning, it ultimately spelled the end for Jobs at Apple.

Our concern here is not the rehashing of failed relationships but rather teaching the importance of being able to spot a bad one and then showing how you can deal with it. Here are six clues to a failed relationship:

1. *Instinctive avoidance.*

Sales managers know that when they stop making eye contact with a salesperson, "termination" has already set in. Through excuses that seem believable, we find ways to avoid eye contact, speaking, or meeting altogether. These often subconscious reactions sound plausible and can put off the termination of a relationship for long periods of time: the serviceperson who is always in the field avoiding the manager; the spouse who has too many meetings or a hectic travel schedule.

2. *Taking pleasure in another person's foul-ups, failures, and foibles.*

It feels good when you learn of another person's mistake; you get a kick out of her slip-up; you enjoy it when he stumbles. You laugh too heartily at her forgetfulness.

3. *Focusing on the negative.*

You can tell if a relationship is shaky when either you or the other person increasingly puts the other down. You see the negative in whatever the other person does. If someone is late to meetings, you call that fact to his attention. Or he may comment on your management style, saying: "She's too soft (or too tough); nothing ever comes of his meetings; she just thinks we're her slaves."

4. *Exaggerated response.*

Minor mistakes turn into World War III. "How could you leave me standing here waiting for you for ten minutes?" "That report was due today, at 5:00 P.M., not 6:00 P.M." "You mess everything up, I just can't depend on you."

5. *Hard to give recognition.*

Praising someone you don't like takes on a quality of hypocrisy; recognizing that person's good work seems impossible. You choke when you try to praise him or her, even when the deed is outstanding. Instead, you have fantasies about one-upping the person.

6. *Experiencing time together as draining.*

Over dinner, for instance, conversation may seem halting, and you struggle to reclaim the magic. The sharing of thoughts about the day or the future seems fruitless. After spending time with the person, you feel worse about yourself rather than better. At best you are bored, at worst you are angry. Your thoughts become negative and you may feel tired. You have a sense of relief (and have a desire for fresh air) when the meal is over.

THE CLAIMING PROCESS:
TERMINATE OR MANAGE

When any relationship shows signs of not working, the mature thing to do is to admit the problem and manage the relationship or terminate it. Like many of our concepts, this one runs contrary to popular thought. Often we are told that it's better to hang in there, never give up hope. So you will be doing lots of denying and procrastinating before you reach the breaking point. You assume that it will get better, that the other person will change, that it won't really affect you, but negative relationships take as much management as, or more than, positive ones.

A negative relationship will block your strengths.

A computer salesperson once told us he made the mistake of calling his boss, the general sales manager, on a stupid policy. The manager has made the salesperson's life miserable from then on. "I'm overlooked for promotions, my expense reports are scrutinized, new product updates are late getting to me, my support person has been transferred after three years." Is anyone winning in that situation? No.

Terminate: Terminating a relationship is often the best move. You may have to fire an employee, quit your job, get a divorce, or get out of a contract. The goal is to swiftly end all contact. It is like a poison that spoils all the good that exists.

Manage: A troubled relationship may not require termination but management instead. Management might include a transfer to a different office of the same company, a change in the way you communicate with the person, or a different job description. In a managed situation, the relationship is restructured so both parties stop damaging each other.

A good relationship, at any level, is an ongoing process that allows your strengths to develop. It enriches your life and helps to cushion you against loss.

One of the reasons why relationships sometimes fail is that they start off with the wrong expectations, the topic of our next chapter.

CHAPTER 7

Nothing Happens Until Someone Expects Something of You in Ways You Can Achieve

General Norman Schwarzkopf was on his way to the shower in his Tampa home on the evening of August 1, when the hot-line phone in his bedroom rang. It was Colin Powell, chairman of the Joint Chiefs of Staff, ordering his old friend to fly up to Washington in time for a meeting two days hence. Schwarzkopf would meet with more than 350 military strategists, Powell, and, ultimately, the President himself. The question? Was Schwarzkopf the man to lead Operation Desert Shield?

The genius of Powell's choice is now history. Not only did he correctly pick Schwarzkopf as the man to lead America and the allies in Operation Desert Shield, but he set an expectation for the general that changed his life forever.

EVERY DAY, IN A THOUSAND DIFFERENT WAYS, WE ARE TOLD WHAT IS EXPECTED OF US

Think back to your board of directors in Chapter 6. How many of those people expected something of you, expected you to achieve something? If you're like most people, the answer is all of them.

Phil Esposito, former Stanley Cup player and center for the Boston Bruins of the National Hockey League, talks about the expectations set for him early in life. His earliest memories are of his mother getting up well before dawn to make breakfast and help pack his hockey equipment onto the toboggan he used to carry his gear through the snow to the local rink. "She was always there, supporting and cheering me on at games and practice meets. My dad was there for me, too, in a quieter way. There were times when my dad had maybe $2.50 or $3.00 in his pocket and rather than use that money to go to the movies, he'd buy my brother, Tony, and me a hockey stick."

Years later, when Phil was out on the ice, playing in the Stanley Cup championship, what was he thinking about?

- They invested in me.

- I can't let her down.

- I'll never have another chance like this to show them what I can do.

Those thoughts are precisely what makes expectations so valuable for achieving goals and playing your strengths to the maximum.

For young Phil, every strength—emotional, mental, and physical—was rigged to fulfill those expectations.

Expectations, however, have an equally powerful flip side.

Several years ago, we worked with one of the top insurance agencies in the Midwest. At the time, their most promising new agent was a retired army officer who, from his résumé, appeared set to become one of the agency's top producers. He was a paratrooper, had an MBA from Harvard, a distinguished military record, great command of the language, and was on a first-name basis with hundreds of military personnel in the area. His manager had great expectations for him and told him so.

He worked hard. He made a lot of sales presentations, but virtually none of them turned into sales. His manager asked him to tape his next presentation so he could find out why. When they listened to the tape, he did almost everything right. He made a first-rate impression as he highlighted the benefits, described the various policies, and listened for the customer's needs. But when it came time to ask for the order, he choked. His speech would speed up, and instead of asking for the order, he would launch into a new round of sales talk. He exhausted himself and his clients but made no sales. His manager diagnosed his problem. "He can't close."

After several months of training in closing techniques, very little changed. Instead of accepting that insurance sales wasn't for him, he decided to move on to another agency where "They had more discipline and a better training program." He took his power-packed résumé (plus his newly acquired experience in the insurance world) and landed a spot with another top agency. In the first few weeks, he was encouraged by a few sales, but once the extensive hand-holding stopped, the "choke" syndrome flared up again. Did he quit? Of course not. He was admonished to keep planning his work and "working his plan." He worked even harder. But after a year of intense effort, in a pressure-packed agency filled with top performers, he ended up in the hospital with a bleeding ulcer. He never returned to the insurance field. Today he runs a thriving and successful equestrian farm in the Midwest where he doesn't have to ask for an order.

Wrong expectations, the belief that he could sell, nearly killed the officer. The wrong expectations can and often do destroy people every day. Luckily, he made the transition to a field in which the expectations were in tune with his strengths. Unfortunately, many people, particularly those who buy into the belief that anything can be accomplished as long as you work hard enough, end up by losing. Strong expectations by those who sincerely care about you can destroy you, when those expectations don't fit your strengths. In this chapter we want to show how, with the right expectations, a person can achieve excellence and how, with the wrong expectations, a person can be destroyed.

GREAT EXPECTATIONS:
WHAT I EXPECT OF MYSELF

Most of us deal with two sets of demands, internal and external. Internal demands are our thoughts, desires, and attitudes that tell us what we want and need. External demands come from the world at large. Internal expectations grow out of the hundreds of statements we hear in our formative years from parents, friends, co-workers, managers, and society at large. As we hear them, we accept or reject them. Ultimately they become vivid, mental photographs of how we see ourselves and what we want to become. We all have a snapshot for:

- How you need to be perceived by others.
  Are you honest, hard-working, chic, intelligent, clever, a valued friend, or capable parent?

- How good you need to be.
  Is your goal to do a good job, or do you need to be the best in whatever you do?

- How much money you need to make.
  Do you need to be "living within your means," or do you need to create a seven-figure estate?

- What type of home you need.
  Are you content with a one-bedroom apartment,

a three-bedroom ranch, or do your expectations demand a "mansion"?

- What type of car you need to drive.
  Is basic transportation your goal, or do you feel complete only if you're driving a Ford truck, a station wagon, or a Jaguar?

- What title you need to have.
  Is your identity defined as an "owner," a doctor, a vice president, or a manager?

- What type of family you need to have.
  Is your picture completed by a spouse and three children, or do you define yourself as the independent self-sufficient single?

- Whom you need to associate with.
  Do you need to fraternize with corporate leaders, sports heroes, and politicians, or do you find satisfaction working with the disadvantaged?

- What you need to do to feel you're making a significant contribution.
  Do you need to be working for the Peace Corps, running a company, serving your country, or raising a family?

I KNOW YOU CAN DO IT:
THE EXPECTATIONS OF OTHERS

My darling Boy:

Beyond "Congratulations, Congressman," what can I say to my dear son in this hour of triumphant success? In this as in all the many letters I have written you there is the same theme: I love you, I believe in you: I expect great things of you.

To me your election not only gratifies my pride as a mother in a splendid and satisfying son and delights me with the realization of the joy you must feel in your success, but it in a measure compensates for the heartache and disappointment I experienced as a child when my dear father lost the race you have just won. My confidence in the good judgment of the people was sadly shattered then by their choice of another. Today my faith is restored. How happy it would have made my precious noble father to know that the first born of his first born would achieve the position he desired! It makes me happy to have you carry on the ideals and principles so cherished by that great and good man. I gave you his name. I commend to you his example. You have always justified my expectations, my hopes, my dreams. How dear to me you are you cannot know, my darling boy, my devoted son, my strength and comfort. Take care of yourself, darling. Write to me. Always re-

(From *The Presidents' Mothers* by Doris Faber, New York: St. Martin's Press, 1968.)

member that I love you and am behind you in all that comes to you. Kiss my dear children in Washington for me.

> My dearest love,
> Mother

In this letter from Lyndon Johnson's mother to him following his election to Congress, her expectations for his success are clear.

External motivations are built on the messages we hear daily:

"Son, I know you can do it."

"We're behind you all the way."

"This is just the beginning."

"What a great idea, I hope you do it."

"I'll be back for your graduation."

"I'm looking forward to reading your book."

"At this rate, you'll be salesman of the year."

"Second best is a loser."

The expectation of achieving, of being somebody, nearly always grows out of a special type of relationship, one that is positive and caring. The most achieving people grow out of caring relationships, such as with parents, in which you know that no matter what, the person is always there expecting the best for you.

In a 1960–61 study of high-achieving financial

consultants in Manhattan, it was noted that a significant percentage of them lost family wealth in the stock
market crash of 1929. Their mothers, however, never
let them forget their pre-crash lifestyle. "We didn't always live like this" was an oft-repeated phrase, as were
comments about the "good china, linen, and silver-
ware." They were compelled to find a way to live up to
the rich and noble lifestyle that they were expected to
attain.

Partners also set expectations. In Paula's case, a
former partner set a major expectation in motion. "One
Saturday, after the sale of Infonics in the early seventies,
I met with two of my former associates to do some
brainstorming. Among the ideas proposed was the possibility of launching a publishing venture. We kicked
around various ideas and landed on the idea of publishing a book on women and money." A number of potential writers were suggested, but before the short list was
completed, George Otis, a former member of the Infonics board and longtime friend, interrupted.

"Paula, I can't think of anyone better suited to
write a book on women and money than you."

"I can't write a book, George."

"Of course you can, you're a great writer. I've read
dozens of your letters and proposals."

"Do you really think so?"

"You bet."

Knowing that George had successfully written more than eight books in the Christian market and had known her and her work for years, she took him at his word. At that moment two ideas were set in motion: a powerful expectation that Paula would write a book and, simultaneously, the permission to try. "George's words were so motivational that within two hours of our lunch I was back in my office dictating what amounted to the first draft of my first book, *The Joy of Money,* which sold over 500,000 copies."

So far, we've been talking about the positive expectations of others. There are three other equally powerful categories.

NEGATIVE EXPECTATIONS

Negative expectations grow out of projecting what a person cannot do rather than building on his or her strengths.

- Don't be ridiculous, you can't do that.

- That's for rich folks, not people like us.

- You're no John Kennedy.

- They're not looking for someone from nowhere.

- You're no Harvard MBA.

LOW EXPECTATIONS

Low expectations are rooted in stereotyping, sexism, and racism. People are seen and judged in terms of what they're doing versus what their strengths may allow them to do.

- She's just a secretary—what does she know about mergers and acquisitions?

- He's just a college kid—what can he know about selling million-dollar deals?

- You don't have the experience to apply for that job.

- You don't have the education to run for office.

WRONG EXPECTATIONS

When no match exists between expectations and strengths, the result is wrong expectations. Often these assumptions grow out of popular beliefs that are also wrong.

- Salespeople should be good at paperwork.

- People should be able to sell because they've attended a sales seminar.

- A child should be as good as his sister or brother in school.

- People should succeed because they went to the right school, have the right look, or have a "perfect résumé."

- People should live up to another person's standards rather than their own standards.

- People should achieve quotas because they have been assigned them.

- Others should think the same way we think.

WHO WE ARE AND WHOM WE WANT TO BE: CLOSING THE GAP

When you combine your internal and external images, you feel a craving to be that person. You create an image of the person you want to be. The clearer the image, the more likely you are to become whom you imagine. If the craving is to become a vice president of the firm, nothing short of that will satisfy that need.

If your craving is to find the cure for AIDS or the source of electricity, nothing but the discovery will satisfy you.

That craving is created by the difference between *who you are and whom you want to be,* or between the real self and the ideal self. The greater the difference or dissonance, the greater your motivation (except when the gap is so great that the person feels the goal can never be achieved).

SETTING YOURSELF UP FOR SUCCESS: EMPOWERING STRENGTHS WITH THE RIGHT EXPECTATIONS

When a perfect match of expectations, relationships, strengths, and rewards exists, you have a recipe for success. An expectation must:

1. Be based on an existing strength.

2. Be shared with a person who cares about your success.

3. Be aligned both internally and externally.

4. Contain an anticipated reward.

Right Expectations Are Based on Strengths

The right expectations begin from the inside out. When you are familiar with your strengths, you can use them to fulfill your expectations. So you must be sure that as you shape your expectations, you consider what your strengths are. You may want to go back to Chapter 3 and review the five characteristics of a strength. Or use the following quiz to test for "it," your strength:

1. Do you feel you always knew how to do *it*?

2. When you practice it, do you get better at *it*?

3. Do you know you can perform *it* well?

4. Do others applaud you when you do *it*?

5. Can you get paid well for doing *it*?

6. Do you feel pride and pleasure when you do *it*?

If you answered yes to all six, you are building on a strength. If you indicated yes to fewer than four, you may not be. Instead, you may be a victim of fantasy strengths.

Strengths: Real or Fantasy

In our culture, it is not unusual to know people whom we call "want to's," those who "want to" write the Great American Novel, become a millionaire, or win a gold medal at the Olympics. While their expectations are at work, they talk without trying, dream without doing. They learn to look the part without being the part.

- In Texas, they may dress like a rich rancher in ostrich boots and a Stetson.

- In Los Angeles, they may rent a Mercedes and talk of their next "deal."

- In New York, they may wear the $2,000 Brioni suit and make references to the next merger.

Like a great actor, "want-to's" adopt the trappings of their dream perfectly. We call this "big hat, no cattle." Mostly it is a result of dreams without the talent to match. Or it can be based on the ultimate tragedy: believing that the world will provide for you.

Here's how you can tell if you're pursuing false expectations:

1. You have the trappings of success but nothing behind them.

2. You are taking no steps to achieve your goal.

3. You have learned the ABCs of a field but you make little progress.

It's often tough to admit you're on a fantasy track. When you finally do, you may suffer a momentary loss (a few months to a year), but when you start down a new track armed with your true strengths (as with the officer you met several pages back), your life will be a thousand times more satisfying.

Share Your Expectation with a Trusted Friend: The Power of Awareness

The most powerful expectations can be created only between two people: you and your manager; you and your partner; you and your subordinate; you and the members of your family. When you tell someone who cares about you that you intend to earn a master's degree, run the marathon, become division manager, or acquire a company, the expectation generates a new energy. We want to live up to our friends' expectations. True, leaders can set goals, as did President Kennedy with his "ask not" Inauguration Address and Bush with his "thousand points of light." But while those words are remembered and recorded, rarely do they move us to act. Only when one person shares with a person of significance to her that she is going to provide shelter for a hundred homeless persons in her community does a point of light begin to shine.

The Power of Awareness

Traditionally, most self-help books present the goal-setting process like this: Set a personal goal, write it down, and add all the ideas necessary to make it work. Great advice, but it leads us to setting goals in a vacuum. The missing agent is the sharing of a goal with another person. That way, by knowing that someone else is expecting you to achieve, you will feel compelled to take action.

Goals remain dreams until they are shared with someone who cares about you.

Your career board of directors, discussed in Chapter 6, is an effective place to share your goals.

We call this sharing the awareness process. It sounds simple, and it is—two people merely talking to each other. When we began this book, an expectation was set in motion for its completion and its success. When a person decides to run for President, he shares that confidence with his closest advisors and friends. Once that announcement is made at the press conference, the expectation die is cast. A spoken expectation is a commitment; once set, it whispers to you: "Now you have to come through."

The Expectations Game: Matching Internal and External Expectations

Your internal and external expectations are in alignment when *others expect you to do what you want to do*. For instance:

- They want you to file, and you like to file.

- Others want you to sell, and you love to sell.

- Others want you to teach, and you love to teach.

You are out of alignment when what others want you to do is *not* what you want to do. When that happens, your body becomes your barometer. You feel resistance, stress, perhaps fatigue. In this case, it is impossible for the expectations of either party to be met in the long run. While there will be attempts to get you to like filing, or selling, or teaching, it's unlikely that will happen. The end result? Everyone loses.

In marriages, this misalignment is at its peak when the wife wants to go out on the town and the husband is perfectly content watching *Monday Night Football*.

Could it be that people are not successes or failures but merely individuals in the right or wrong expectation environment?

His social expectations are met, hers are not. The two don't fit. A similar situation can happen between partners or co-workers when expectations about the other person are out of alignment with his or her strengths. It's not that one person is right or wrong, good or bad; it's simply that the alignment is wrong. This raises an interesting question. *Does failure truly exist, or is it simply an inaccurate matchup of expectations and strengths? Could it be that people are not successes or failures but merely individuals in the right or wrong expectation environment?*

Be Careful Whom You Partner With

If your goal is to write a book, you'll want to align with people who are supportive of that activity and know something about it. If you want to travel around the world, it makes no sense to spend time with stay-at-homes or people who want to discuss the details of the latest airplane crash. If you want to win an election, don't waste your time converting people from one party to another. Instead, the political sophisticates concentrate on getting those who already believe in them to the voting booths. But how often do we put ourselves in mismatched situations in which the goal is to change the other person? *Don't look to change the expectations and attitudes of others, look for the right alignment from the beginning.* People are who they are. Play to their strengths!

Clearly Visualize and Anticipate the Reward

The fourth step, reward, comes in a variety of forms. For Joe Montana, it's Superbowl V. For the next President, it's inauguration day and the opportunity to make a difference. For Olympic athletes, it's winning a gold medal. For others it may be parties, celebrations, money, prestige, titles, new offices and opportunities. But reward is not only the punch line to an expectation, it is also the pleasure you derive from working toward a goal. It is so powerful that we are devoting the final chapter of the book to the topic.

Expectations: A Moving Target

Expectations are exciting because they move us toward the goal of whom we want to be. But as we close in on this goal, something magical happens—it inevitably moves forward a bit. Often, it becomes larger or changes composition altogether. For instance, if your goal is to build an estate of $1 million, suddenly when you approach your first goal, the ante gets upped to $2 million. Or if you want to become Vice President and the title seems within reach, suddenly you like the idea of becoming President better. Because of this "moving target," your life will always have some dissonance. But a tolerable amount of dissonance is a good thing. In growing lives, there is always an "element of discontent." Anytime a goal is satisfied, the dissonance is lost, as is the drive that pushes you forward. We've seen this phenomena when entrepreneurs, for instance, sell or merge their companies. Often they are left with a feeling of emptiness or a sense that all their goals have been achieved. They are experiencing the loss of that dissonance—there is nothing left for them to strive for. But new expectations can inspire them by offering a new set of challenges.

As was discussed in Chapter 5, when there is a life mission there is always more to do. Tending your mission keeps you focused on the future, and this provides fertile ground for new and exciting goals that can be turned into expectations, for we are forever changing as we grow.

> The future is not a result of choices among alternative paths offered by the present, but a place that is created —created first in mind and will, created next in activity. The future is not some place we are going to, but one we are creating. The paths to it are not found but made, and the activity of making them changes both the maker and the destination.
>
> —John Schaar

CHAPTER 8

Celebration: The Way to Recognize Good Work

In the closing pages of *Don't Shoot, It's Only Me,* Bob Hope's best-selling memoir about his fifty years in show business, he answers this question:

"After all these years, why don't you retire and go fishing?"

"I would, but fish don't applaud."

Curious, isn't it, how even the likes of Bob Hope are hooked by the power of applause? Everyone wants his special achievements to be celebrated, from anniversaries to promotion. Knowing how powerful that elixir is, it's shocking to see how overlooked it is in most areas of life, especially business and education. Consider what people have done for recognition even if only for Andy Warhol's famous fifteen minutes: camped out atop flagpoles, gulped down goldfish, raced motorcycles over the tops of cars, walked across America, descended Niagara Falls in a barrel, and even committed grave atrocities.

In our experience, we have never seen a person who has suffered from overrecognition. People may be damaged by being manipulated with flattery, but it may be impossible to give too much praise for achievement. If it was possible, the likes of Bob Hope should have been destroyed long ago. Instead, they seem to get better and better.

Think how devastating it can be when a special day for you isn't celebrated. You don't feel recognized. What happens to a little five-year-old whose parents forget to celebrate her birthday or the Vietnam vets who looked forward to a hero's welcome only to be greeted with boos and rotten eggs? The result is broken spirits, broken relationships, and smashed expectations.

Our goal in this chapter is to cast new light on the practice of celebration as a catalyst for inspiring your strengths and those of other people. This is a note to naysayers: If you believe all that "hoopla stuff" is fluff, our message is "stay tuned." To miss this point is to miss the strengths' message entirely.

While it's true that some great work may be accomplished in isolation, true magic happens when there's celebration for it. Our studies repeatedly show that individual performances soar when good work is celebrated. In 1986, Nancy Philips, who was clearly a whiz at the computer keyboard, moved into a data entry position at SRI Gallup. After several months, we put in a computerized measurement program to track the number of strokes inputted each month. Nancy logged in at 550,000 strokes per month (50 percent above the national average). At a monthly awards program, where employees are celebrated for personal bests and top performance in more than thirty categories, she received her first round of applause. "After winning that first award, I was sure I could do one million strokes." Three months later she reached her goal. Not long afterward, Nancy found she had punched 112,000 strokes in one day. She quickly multiplied that to 2 million strokes per month, a figure she exceeded six months later. Most people would be content with this world-record production, but not Nancy. "I'm real competitive. I love knowing I'm the best and that I've become a model for others." At last count, Nancy had been celebrated more than forty-eight times. Today her personal best is 3,526,000 strokes in one month. (We claim her to be the world's best data entry person, and no one has yet challenged us.) Nancy Philips is a product of the right expectations being set and then celebrated.

Several years back, we conducted a survey of the employees of the Data Documents plant and found only 6 percent felt they had received adequate recognition. Data Documents' senior management decided to remedy the situation. They brainstormed the topic for more than eight hours, coming up with ideas they could put into practice at the next monthly meeting. As a follow-up, we conducted a survey to determine the effectiveness of the changes. In six months, 57 percent of the employees felt they were now receiving positive recognition for their work. But not only did the perception change, so did the results. Without being worked on directly, efficiency and productivity improved significantly as the recognition increased.

CELEBRATION: MORE THAN CAKES AND CHRISTMAS PARTIES

In the largest sense, *people are attracted to that which is celebrated, and people do what they are celebrated for.*

Consider that line for a moment. In the sixties, at the time of Sputnik and Gemini, it was the engineers who were taking the bows, and graduate schools around the country were turning out mechanical and electrical engineers like hotcakes. In the seventies, the spotlight landed on journalists like Woodward and Bernstein as they chronicled Watergate. Again, students crammed into journalism classes. In the eighties, the ever-moving target hit Wall Street, and the MBA mills are still churning out B-school grads.

The spotlight, it seems, is always on sports. In many states, such as Texas, Oklahoma, and Nebraska, for example, football is raised to the level of a religion. In Lincoln on a football Saturday, the town becomes one "Go Big Red" event as nearly 80,000 fans pack the stadium to cheer on the Huskers. As a result, there is nary a young boy in Nebraska who doesn't have a Cornhusker hero or doesn't long to be on the team when he grows up.

In Italy, the same adulation is granted to opera stars and soccer players. In Britain cheers are heard for cricket players. (Think how many kids might start lusting after science and math as a career if the same recognition and celebration were accorded those professions.)

Celebration does not merely happen in the form of applause and plaques. It is most valuable when it happens on a variety of levels.

THE MANY FACES OF CELEBRATION

Speaking

Most people would rather be punished than ignored. By not speaking to another person, we are ignoring his or her existence. The simple act of one person speaking to another is the first way to celebrate the person's existence. By speaking, you are saying "Hello, human being." As basic as speaking is, it is not uncommon for a new person to join a company and feel like an outsider simply because few people even offer a hello. The odds of a company keeping employees improve significantly when people are celebrated and acknowledged by name in their first hours at a new position. People prefer to go places where they are recognized, where they are known. Just as children do not want to go to parties where they do not know anyone, adults do not like to work where they are "strangers."

Watching

As you watch, you take a mental photograph of what a person does. Like listening, watching is a form of recognition and appreciation. We see this in children begging "Watch me, watch me" as they play soccer, dress dolls, stack blocks, play Little League, or dive off a diving board.

That longing doesn't disappear with the years. The experience of watching a furniture craftsman or an artist is one of sheer fascination and pleasure for the beholder and the subject. Or we watch Olympic events and dramatic performances. But watching can apply to us all. "Come see my office, come meet my co-workers, come see my new computer." All are requests for celebration and recognition. What salesperson wouldn't love a choir of people observing her greatest sales presentation? What auto mechanic doesn't relish an audience as he diagnoses what's wrong with an engine? Watching is a pleasurable experience, one that implies appreciation and bolsters strengths. However, it must not be thought of as a time to criticize.

Speaking and watching may appear basic. They are. So basic, in fact, that without them, all the following ways of celebrating are meaningless. Let us repeat: Individuals and organizations that don't respect the first two steps of celebration will find these more sophisticated steps inconsequential. The reason? Celebration is a building-block process. If people do not feel like human beings all during the year, a year-end bonus check will ring hollow, a year-end Christmas party will seem hypocritical.

Writing

For many, the written word has a value and power superior to the spoken word since it allows for fuller expression. In 1970 we printed a card shaped like a drop of water. We called it "A Drop for Your Bucket." These were made available for associates to write positive comments on and give to associates to compliment them on their work or behavior. Positive comments were "bucket fillers." This has become an ongoing way for associates to celebrate each other. Our observation is that people do enjoy recognizing each other. A good system such as the "drop" helps them do it.

Reward and Recognition

Peer recognition is the most powerful form of celebration. When an equal acknowledges your performance, you feel respected and sense that your work is fully appreciated.

In focus groups with professional athletes, we ask about the best recognition they receive. You might expect they will say the thousands of cheering fans. They do not. Rather, they say their favorite recognition is the slap on the butt or the hug they get from a teammate when they make a stellar play. It's immediate and authentic.

In 1990 Dr. Lee Salk, the noted child psychologist, was awarded an SRI Hall of Fame Award. When a fellow psychologist made the presentation, he said, "Every hundred years there is a great mind in a particular field, and Dr. Lee Salk is just one of those great minds in the field of child psychology. He can think about what is right for children better than any other person in the world or in our century." It was an extraordinary moment to behold as one peer recognized another.

To be truly effective, recognition must be tailored to the particular person. Some people appreciate financial rewards, others like an audience of family and peers, while others would more value publicity in the leading local newspaper or in an industry magazine.

THE ROLE OF MEASUREMENT
IN CELEBRATION

Measurement is at the heart of virtually every aspect of our lives, from the scores on *Monday Night Football* to our body weight. It's the process by which we keep track of where we are and how we measure up. It is the gauge by which the Academy Awards and the People's

Choice Awards are determined. It is the yardstick by which the Super Bowl is won or lost.

Winning and losing in the corporate world are rarely based on anything so scientific. On the one hand, bottom-line decisions are stressed and measurement in the financial area is expected to be pinpoint accurate. But there is almost no measurement of individual performance. The result? The perks and applause too often go to the brownnosers and corporate politicians instead of the top performers.

The year-end bonus is an example of a good idea gone wrong.

Recently, we heard this bonus story from a twenty-seven-year-old fast-climbing Manhattan bank executive. "Last December, I got my bonus check, opened it, eyed the amount, and walked into my boss's office and said, 'If this is your idea of a bonus, I would rather not have it.'" Two days later a check for $5,000, not $1,000, arrived on his desk.

Despite his short-term win, he understandably felt it a hollow victory. In his situation, the manager had $20,000 in bonus money to divide among ten people. His decision was not based on performance but personality. The winner was the "yes man," the person who played up to the manager or occasionally, like our friend, the one who complained the loudest. What kind of reward is that? Instead of being a celebration of a strength, it becomes a political game. In no way does it show what a real champion you are. If your work deserves celebrating, then it must be able to be measured.

The process of measurement can be broken down into four categories:

Count it: This is measuring performance based on quantity: sales made, numbers added, units produced, pages typed, bumpers assembled, mergers completed, laps run, miles driven. With this data you can compare personal growth from one month to the next, one quarter to the next, one year to the next. It is, above all, data from which two or more people can draw the same conclusion.

Rate it: At Fairfield Inn operated by Marriott, customers are asked to rate the quality of hospitality based on a point scale. At Federal Express, the employees rate their managers on a point scale. When used over a period of time, this type of rating can tell who objectively deserves recognition.

Rank it: Billboard Magazine hails the Top 100, *The New York Times* lists the top-ten best sellers in fiction and nonfiction, *Forbes* ranks the four hundred richest people in the world, and *Fortune Magazine* ranks its Fortune 500. In business and industry, the most common ranking is for salespeople. In sales within a company there is always a number-one producer based on dollar volume, a number two, and a number three. Interestingly, there may be many significant gaps between the dollar amounts, but they are still the top three producers. This type of ranking is possible for many job categories, from support people to engineering to management, yet few organizations use it.

Target it: The measurement is binary, achieved or not achieved. The report was completed by June 12 or it was not. The building was completed or not. The person was recruited and hired or was not. When there is a bull's-eye, there is reason to celebrate.

Measurement would put an end to the days of the sugar daddies and game players. Hallelujah! Think what we could have: authentic celebration for authentic achievement.

THE CELEBRATION PROCESS: GETTING THE APPLAUSE YOU NEED

Every family and organization has a different celebration style. Some are serious and formal while others are spontaneous and casual. Whatever your environment, the most essential step is for you to understand your own need for recognition and find ways to fulfill it.

Here are several questions to guide you:

1. Are you getting enough recognition out of your current work environment?
   Compensation
   Inclusion in the decision-making process
   Recognition from your boss and peers
   Appreciation from customers

2. What two or three ways of being recognized can you expect in the next two to three years?
   Personal attention from the boss
   A bigger office
   A party given for you by your friends
   A larger paycheck
   Opportunities to use your strengths
   A more impressive title
   Customer compliments
   More responsibility
   Your ideas will count more

3. How do you get more?
   Make sure you are using your strengths
   Talk with your boss
   Help other people achieve

Do more/sell more

Give more than you take

Make the right political moves

Build more one-to-one relationships

Make sure other people are getting ample recognition

Develop your competencies

4. If you're not getting the recognition you deserve where you are, what can you do?

Is it possible to get it here?

Do you need to move to a company where they give more recognition?

Do you need to join a volunteer organization?

Can you develop new skills that could be recognized?

Do you need to give more recognition to others?

Celebrate Your Strengths

"I don't need any rewards, that stuff's not for me." For many people the idea of rewarding themselves is unthinkable. "Oh, I couldn't do that." If that sounds like you, you will want to rethink your attitude. As we have shown, personal rewards are an important part of strengths-building. They can take many forms. Examples are throwing a small, elegant dinner party (for yourself or your personal board of directors) when you close a big deal, or purchasing a $150 Mont Blanc pen when you are promoted. Some may call this self-indulgent. We call it strengths-building. Highly successful people reward themselves as a matter of course. In a study of customer attitudes for a luxury hotel chain, we found that people who spend $300 to $400 a night for a hotel room do so because they feel they "deserve it." The same is true for those of us who spend a week at Palm Aire, a day at Elizabeth Arden, dine at The Four Seasons, or break open a bottle of Chateau Lafite Rothschild. We do it because we deserve it.

Find or Create Ways to Celebrate Strengths

A life filled with celebration is a rich one indeed. If celebration is not a part of your work, you could find a reason for it in your family or community. Organizations such as the Boy Scouts, Girl Scouts, and the Business and Professional Women's Organization are places where achievement is regularly celebrated. On a community level, the Rotary Club, the Lions, and Kiwanis celebrate civic deeds on a weekly basis.

Many companies, including Apple, IBM, and 3M, are famous for their recognition programs. They know that if you want to improve the performance of others, applaud them by letting them know how good they are. Sheri Hirst, former head of special projects for Occidental Petroleum Chairman Armand Hammer, is a giver who understands the value of celebrating the strengths of her friends. As a matter of course, she clips newspaper articles on friends and sends along a congratulatory note. She always sends flowers to co-workers, friends, and business associates to congratulate them on a job well done.

Another way to celebrate other people's strengths is to suggest that they write a book, give a speech, run for public office, or be honored as volunteer of the year. Recommending others for jobs or honorary positions is also a good idea. Note: Never celebrate someone without involving his or her "primary audience": family, friends, or spouse. To be honored alone is a lovely experience, but it can be lonely.

THE GREATEST NIGHT OF MY LIFE

The site was New York City and the celebration was for the managers of Harman Management, one of the largest KFC franchisors with over two hundred stores. The spot was the Rainbow Room atop Rockefeller Center.

As the group was walking to Rockefeller Center, someone asked who was going to be the party's entertainment. "Johnny Desmond."

"Who?" people asked.

It became apparent that the young people were hoping for Michael Jackson, not Johnny Desmond. Some griped, but one young manager said, "Johnny Desmond is going to be there tonight. We cannot change that. What we can do is *be the best audience Johnny Desmond has ever had.*"

That idea was contagious.

So for song after song, the audience clapped and cheered. Desmond got better and better, singing as he had not sung in years. For the finale, he sang "New York, New York." The audience exploded in a standing ovation. Johnny Desmond, his face wet with tears, walked out into the audience, hugged people, and said, "This is the greatest night of my life!"

ACKNOWLEDGMENTS

Every book has a band of people who help make it happen and this one is no different. It is to these catalysts and supporters that we express our appreciation for helping to make *Soar with Your Strengths* a reality:

The Catalysts

Joyce Caldwell

Jonathan Lazear

Wendy Lazear

Jennifer Flannery

Bob Shook

Robert Heady

Leslie Schnur

The Supporters

Marcus Buckingham

Bob Gordman

Elie Gordman

Cary Ross

Fred Dobbs

Shirley Clifton

Connie Rath

Ellen Hoeppner

Lee Salk

Larry Hadfield

JoAnn Aggens

Loretta Hatton

Glenna Dorais

Sherry Bush

Sheri Hirst

Denise Cavanaugh

Lyn Weidman

Jack Weidman

Frank Brown

Lady Windemere